3

Reading for a Reason
Expanding Reading Skills

Laurie Blass
Elizabeth Whalley

Reading for a Reason Student Book 3: Expanding Reading Skills

Published by McGraw-Hill ESL/ELT, a business unit of The McGraw-Hill Companies, Inc. 1212 Avenue of the Americas, New York, NY 10020. Copyright © 2006 by The McGraw-Hill Companies, Inc. All rights reserved. No part of this publication may be reproduced or distributed in any form or by any means, or stored in a database or retrieval system, without the prior written consent of The McGraw-Hill Companies, Inc., including, but not limited to, in any network or other electronic storage or transmission, or broadcast for distance learning.

ISBN: 0-07-294217-7
1 2 3 4 5 6 7 8 9   CCW/CCW   11 10 09 08 07 06 05

Editorial director: Tina Carver
Executive editor: Erik Gundersen
Development editor: Linda O'Roke
Production manager: MaryRose Malley
Photo researchers: David Averbach and Tobi Zausner
Interior designer: Monotype Composition
Cover designer: Monotype Composition

The **McGraw·Hill** Companies

Acknowledgements

The publisher and authors would like to thank the following educational professionals whose comments, reviews, and assistance were instrumental in the development of *Reading for a Reason 3: Expanding Reading Skills*.

► Fairlie Atkinson, Sungkyunkwan University, Seoul, Korea

► Lynne Barsky, Suffolk County Community College, Jericho, NY

► Gerry Boyd, Northern Virginia Community College, Annandale, VA

► Donna Fujimoto, Osaka Jogakuin Daigaku, Osaka, Japan

► Ann-Marie Hadzima, National Taiwan University, Taipei, Taiwan, R.O.C.

► Patricia Heiser, University of Washington, Seattle, WA

► Yu-chen Hsu, National Central University, Taipei, Taiwan, R.O.C.

► Greg Keech, City College of San Francisco, San Francisco, CA

► Irene Maksymjuk, Boston University, Boston, MA

► Yoshiko Matsubayashi, Tokyo International University, Saitama, Japan

► Lorraine Smith, Adelphi University, Garden City, NY

► Leslie Eloise Somers, Miami-Dade County Public Schools, Miami, FL

► Karen Stanley, Central Piedmont Community College, Charlotte, NC

Heartfelt thanks to the McGraw-Hill team, especially Erik Gundersen and Linda O'Roke, who helped shape this series and enhanced our enjoyment of the process.

This book is dedicated to three of the most important teachers in our lives: Harriet Blass, Rafe Chase, and Zorina Wolf.

Table of Contents

Welcome to Reading for a Reason

Reading for a Reason 3: Expanding Reading Skills is the third in a three-level reading series that leads students to develop the critical reading and vocabulary skills they need to become confident, academic readers.

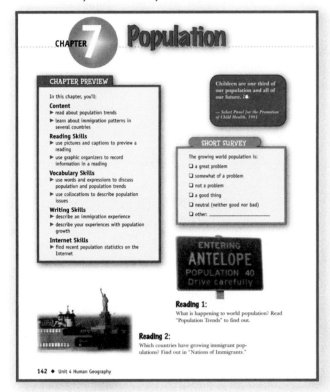

Chapter Preview boxes outline the main goals of the chapter and focus students' attention on what they will learn.

Short Surveys related to the chapter topic help students personalize the chapter content and activate prior knowledge.

Teaser photographs and questions pique students' interest.

Before You Read activities stimulate background knowledge, focus on vocabulary presentation and practice, and introduce important expressions.

Preview activities activate schemata and help students focus on the main idea of the passage.

Vocabulary exercises preview the important words and expressions found in the readings.

The sample page (left, top):

As You Read

As you read, think about this question:
▶ What are the most recent population trends?

🎧 Population Trends

In 1972, the Prime Minister of Singapore asked for zero or even negative population growth. The people of Singapore responded so well that by the mid-1980s, the birth rates were below the level needed to replace the population. He then had to tell the people of Singapore to have more children, "At least two. Better three. Four if you can afford it." The policy reversal in Singapore reflects a population reality: The numbers and distributions of people not yet born are being determined now. Furthermore, the size characteristics, along with the growth trends and migrations of today's populations are features that help shape the well being of people not yet born.

We look at seven aspects of population data—the numbers, age, and sex distribution of people; patterns and trends in their fertility and mortality; their density of settlement and rate of growth—because they affect the social, political and economic organization of a society. In addition, all of these are affected by the social, political, and economic organization of a society, as the Singapore example shows. Through population data, we begin to understand how people in a given area live, how they may interact with one another, how they use the land, what pressure on resources exists, and what the future may bring.

Some Population Patterns

In the 13 years between 1991 and 2004, the earth's population grew from nearly 5.4 billion people to 6.4 billion people. That means that the world population grew about 77 million people annually, or 211,000 people per day. The average, however, conceals the reality that annual increases have been declining over the years. In the early 1990s, the reported yearly growth was 85 million. Even with the slower pace of estimated increase, the United Nations early this century still projected that the world would likely contain nearly 9 billion inhabitants by 2050 and 9.5 billion inhabitants by 2100. It is hard to imagine what these large numbers mean, but some statistics may help you understand. You had lived

146 ◆ Unit 4 Human Geography

Instead of controlling the environment for the benefit of the population, maybe we should control the population to ensure the survival of our environment.
— *Sir David Attenborough (British broadcast journalist, b. 1926)*

ENTERING ANTELOPE POPULATION 40 Drive carefully

As You Read activities present readings that recycle reading skills and vocabulary to build reading fluency and confidence.

Focus questions help students focus while reading, reinforce preview skills, and build schemata.

First reading passages introduce the chapter topic in a short informal reading. Types of texts include emails, newspaper and magazine articles, and textbook excerpts.

The sample page (right, bottom):

After You Read

Comprehension

1. What are the most recent population trends? _____

2. What was the result of the Prime Minister of Singapore's request for zero or even negative population growth? _____

3. What are the seven aspects of population data? _____

4. What happened to the earth's population between 1991 and 2004? _____

5. If annual population increases have been declining each year, why is the Earth's population growing? _____

Talk About It

Discuss these questions.
1. What consequences do you see around you of the increases in population?
2. What can we understand through the study of population data?

What consequences do you see?
I . . .

Chapter 7 Population ◆ 149

After You Read activities focus on the main idea and details presented in Reading 1.

Questions require students to explain important concepts in their own words.

Talk About It activities encourage discussions to help students synthesize, personalize, and extend concepts in the reading.

Welcome to Reading for a Reason ◆ **vii**

The sample page (page 152) contains:

As You Read

As you read, think about this question:
▶ What are some nations with large immigrant populations?

The key problem facing humanity in the coming century is how to bring a better quality of life— for 8 billion or more people—without wrecking the environment entirely in the attempt. 🔹

— *Edward O. Wilson, American biologist, b.1929)*

🎧 Nations of Immigrants

Americans have a belief in a "melting pot" myth and heritage. They are inclined to forget that many other countries are also "nations of immigrants" and that their numbers are dra-
5 matically increasing. In the United States, Canada, Australia, and New Zealand, early colonists from Europe, and later, immigrants from other continents, overwhelmed indigenous populations. In each country, immigra-
10 tion has continued contributing not only to national ethnic mixes but maintaining or enlarging the proportion of the population that is foreign born. In Australia, as one example, that population now equals 25%; in Canada, it is 18%.

The Statue of Liberty

Australia   Canada

Figure 1: *A comparison of the native populations of Australia and Canada*

15 In Latin America, the domination of native people by Europeans was and is less complete and uniform than in Anglo-America. In nearly all South and Central American states, European and other nonnative ethnic groups dominate the social and economic hierarchy. In many countries, however, they constitute

152 ◆ Unit 4 Human Geography

Second reading passages introduce a longer academic, scientific, or formal reading on the chapter topic.

Focus questions help students focus while reading and reinforce prediction skills.

Headings, photographs, figures, and charts in the readings help students practice academic reading skills.

After You Read activities include extended vocabulary practice, reading skills presentation and practice, and collocation practice.

Main Idea questions allow students to check their understanding of the reading.

Getting the Details questions help students identify details, examples, and other types of supporting information in the passage they have just read.

The sample page (page 156) contains:

After You Read

Main Idea
What are some nations with large immigrant populations?

Getting the Details
Answer the following questions. Use complete sentences.

1. What are the main English-speaking countries with large immigrant populations?

2. Where are cross-border movements of migrants and refugees continuing common occurrences?

3. Immigrants and refugees leave because of difficulties in their home countries. What are some of these difficulties?

4. What does the Universal Declaration of Human Rights say about the freedom of individuals to move within or leave their own countries?

5. Do all countries welcome immigrants? Support your answer with examples from the reading.

156 ◆ Unit 4 Human Geography

Using Your Own Graphic Organizer to Take Notes

As you have seen, photographs, diagrams, and drawings help you to understand ideas in a reading. It is often useful to make you own diagrams—or graphic organizers—to help you understand and remember what you read. You can use the graphic organizers that you've seen in previous chapters, or you can design your own. For example, in "Population Trends," you saw a line graph and two pie graphs. Other types of graphs include bar graphs such as the one on page 154.

You can organize information any way that makes sense to you. For example, "Nations of Immigrants" talked about the number of Amerindians in Peru, Bolivia, and Ecuador and the number of European ethnics in Argentina, Uruguay, Costa Rica, and southern Chile. To remember these numbers, you can draw a map of South America and use two kinds of shadings to show the differences or write the numbers on the map itself.

Practice

Use "Nations of Immigrants" on pages 152–155 to make graphic organizers on a separate piece of paper to show the following information.

1. Draw a graphic organizer to show the difference between the numbers of immigrants in Australia and Canada.

2. Use a map of Europe to show the following: "About 20% of Switzerland's populations, 13% of France's, 10% of Sweden's, and over 9% of Germany's are people born outside those countries."

3. Use a graphic organizer to explain the following: "The current rich world is projected to stabilize below 1.5 billion. Poorer countries' numbers will probably be more than 6.5 billion."

Reading Skills boxes present reading comprehension skills needed to succeed in an academic environment.

Reading Skills Practice provides an opportunity for students to learn, practice, and internalize a new skill by using it to interact with the reading passage.

Vocabulary activities provide students with an opportunity to practice additional words and expressions found in Reading 2.

Talk About It activities encourage discussions on questions that help students synthesize, personalize, and extend concepts in the reading.

Vocabulary

A. Here are some more words from "Nations of Immigrants." Find them in the reading and circle them.

Nouns	Verbs	Adjective
enmity	overwhelmed	collective
incidences	recruited	

B. Now use them to complete the sentences.

1. More workers were needed, so guest workers were _____ from Turkey and North Africa. They were invited to immigrate to Europe.

2. The early colonists _____ the indigenous populations. Because they were over-powered, the indigenous populations decreased in number.

3. Some countries had _____ restrictions, which meant that groups of people (for example, Haitians) were not allowed to enter those countries.

4. There were a number of _____ of fighting. These cases of strife pushed residents to become immigrants and leave their homelands

5. The two ethnic groups did not like each other. This _____ made them uncomfortable around each other

Talk About It

Discuss these questions.

1. What surprised you most in the "Nations of Immigrants" reading?

2. How important do you think issues of immigration are in the place where you live?

3. Should people who have no criminal record be free to move to any other country? Why or why not?

What surprised you . . . ?

I didn't know that . . .

Expressions

Collocations for Discussing Nations of Immigrants

Collocations are words that are frequently used together. Here are some collocations from the two readings in this chapter. They relate to population and immigration.

affected by	policies on immigration
(be) a magnet for	rate of growth
distributions of people	right of admittance
policies of exclusion	

Note: These collocations all have prepositions.

Examples:

All of these are **affected by** the social, political and economical organization of a society.

The rich world will increasingly **be a magnet for** those from poorer countries.

Practice

A. Find and underline the collocations from the box above in "Population Trends" and "Nations of Immigrants." As you underline them, pay particular attention to the prepositions in these collocations. Try to memorize them.

B. Now use them to complete the sentences.

1. The _____ indicates the speed at which something is increasing.

2. A country's _____ determine how many people it will let in each year.

3. The _____ are policies that prevent people from entering a country.

4. California _____ immigrants because there are so many opportunities to work on farms.

5. Everyone is _____ the increasing world population because countries are interdependent.

6. It is interesting to look at the _____ in a country. Usually there are more people on the coasts than in the interior of a country.

7. There is no _____. In other words, you cannot move to any country you want.

Expressions presents collocations found in both reading passages and provides students with an opportunity to use them in a contextualized activity.

Internet Research boxes present helpful tips on how to conduct academic research on the Internet.

Write About It activities allow students to write on different but related aspects of the chapter topic.

Internet Research

Learning about Recent Population Statistics on the Internet

You can find a lot of information about population and immigration on the Internet.

For population statistics about the United States, the United States census website is a good source: **www.census.gov/.**

The United States government also keeps statistics on the world population: **www.census.gov/ipc/www/world.html.**

Another source is the nonprofit organization the Population Reference Bureau: **www.prb.org/.**

Because population and immigration trends can change rapidly, the Internet is a good source of up-to-date information.

Practice

Practice finding population and immigration information in the Internet. Find out about any aspect of population and immigration information that interests you or about the following:

► the projected population of the world in 20, 50, and 100 years
► recent population statistics for a country of your choice
► immigration patterns 1920–1950
► immigration patterns 1950–1990
► recent immigration patterns

Share your search experience with the class. On what topic did you do your search? Why did you choose this topic? What keywords did you use? What did you learn that you didn't know about before? If you found interesting photos, diagrams, or graphs, bring them to class.

Write About It

Write about population and immigration. Choose one of these topics:

► Describe how you feel about population growth. How does it affect you personally? Do you feel more crowded than you did three years ago? Where do you feel crowded/not crowded? Does your school have more students? What is your experience?
► Write about an immigration experience of your own or someone you know.

Use five words and expressions from this chapter. Also, try to use your Internet research.

On Your Own is a structured speaking activity that helps students further explore each chapter theme.

Step 1 has students design a survey or prepare a presentation on the chapter topic.

Step 2 asks students to interview classmates using the questions they wrote in Step 1 or give their presentation to the class.

Step 3 allows students to explain the results of their survey or evaluate their presentations.

Wrap Up is an informal assessment tool that reviews chapter content, vocabulary, and reading skills.

Second Timed Reading focuses students' attention on their reading fluency by having them reread Reading 1 and Reading 2 and keep track of their times on the Timed Reading Chart in the back of the book.

Scope and Sequence

Vocabulary Skills	Writing Skills	Internet and Research Skills
▶ Using words and expressions for talking about critical thinking ▶ Using collocations to discuss critical thinking skills	▶ Writing about using critical thinking ▶ Writing about your reading habits	▶ Doing an effective Internet search using keywords ▶ Interviewing classmates about unwarranted assumptions
▶ Using words and expressions for talking about problem solving ▶ Using collocations for discussing creative problem solving	▶ Describing a difficult problem to solve and why it's difficult ▶ Describing a problem you had and how you solved it	▶ Evaluating URLs in search results ▶ Solving a problem as a group
▶ Using words and expressions for talking about written and oral communication in business ▶ Using collocations for discussing business communication	▶ Writing and responding to email ▶ Writing about how you feel about giving oral presentations	▶ Scanning a webpage ▶ Giving an oral presentation
▶ Using words and expressions for talking about ethics and ethics in business ▶ Using collocations to discuss business ethics	▶ Describing an ethical issue you had ▶ Describing your personal code of ethics	▶ Finding and reading corporate codes of ethics on the Internet ▶ Giving an oral presentation on a company's code of ethics
▶ Using words and expressions for talking about film history ▶ Using collocations to discuss film history	▶ Describing your first movie-going experience ▶ Writing about results of an Internet movie search	▶ Learning about film history on the Internet ▶ Interviewing classmates on their favorite classic movie
▶ Using words and expressions for talking about genre films ▶ Using adjectival collocations to discuss genre films	▶ Writing a movie review	▶ Finding movie reviews on the Internet ▶ Giving an oral presentation of a movie review

Scope and Sequence

UNIT 4 — Human Geography

	Text Type/Content	Reading Skills
CHAPTER 7: **Population** page 142	**1:** Human geography textbook excerpt: "Population Trends" **2:** Human geography textbook excerpt: "Nations of Immigrants"	▶ Using Pictures and Captions to Preview a Reading ▶ Using Graphic Organizers to Take Notes
CHAPTER 8: **People and the Environment** page 164	**1:** Magazine article: "The Mystery of Easter Island" **2:** Human geography textbook excerpt: "Cultural Ecology"	▶ Having an Open Mind ▶ Identifying Causes and Effects

UNIT 5 — Biology

	Text Type/Content	Reading Skills
CHAPTER 9: **Cloning** page 188	**1:** Newspaper article: "Cloned Cat is No Copycat" **2:** Biology textbook excerpt: "The Ethics of Cloning"	▶ Putting it all Together to Preview ▶ Forming an Opinion
CHAPTER 10: **Animal Communication** page 210	**1:** Animal behavior textbook excerpt: "Secrets of Cross-species Communication" **2:** Animal behavior textbook excerpt: "How Animals Signal Danger"	▶ Using Your Own Strategies to Preview ▶ Taking Notes to Write a Summary

Vocabulary Skills	Writing Skills	Internet and Research Skills
▶ Using words and expressions to discuss population and population trends ▶ Using collocations to discuss population and immigration	▶ Writing about how population growth affects you personally ▶ Writing about an immigration experience	▶ Finding recent population statistics on the Internet ▶ Presenting research on recent population statistics
▶ Using words and expressions to discuss human interaction with the environment ▶ Using collocations to discuss human impact on the environment	▶ Describing what you are doing to preserve the environment ▶ Describing a lost civilization	▶ Identifying unbiased information on the Internet ▶ Giving an oral presentation on a "lost" civilization
▶ Using words and expressions to discuss cloning ▶ Collocations for discussing cloning	▶ Expressing your opinion on cloning ▶ Expressing your opinion on an ethical issue	▶ Finding news on the Internet ▶ Preparing for a debate on cloning
▶ Using words and expressions to discuss animal and human communication ▶ Collocations for discussing animal communication	▶ Writing about animal communication ▶ Comparing animal and human communication	▶ Finding specific information on a webpage ▶ Giving a presentation on communication

To the Teacher

Series Overview

Reading for a Reason is a three-level academic theme-based reading series that focuses on cross-curricular content and promotes critical thinking skills. The series is designed to enhance the academic reading and vocabulary skills of English language learners. The three books in the series range from High-Beginning to High-Intermediate.

▶ **Reading for a Reason 1**—High-Beginning
Reading passage word count 150–600

▶ **Reading for a Reason 2**—Intermediate
Reading passage word count 425–950

▶ **Reading for a Reason 3**—High-Intermediate
Reading passage word count 550–1500

The objectives of *Reading for a Reason* are to increase students' independence, confidence, competence, and comfort both in reading in English and in learning new vocabulary. To be successful academically, students must have strong reading, vocabulary, and computer skills. *Reading for a Reason* is designed to work on the skills that are most needed for academic success.

To be independent readers, students need to be able to self-activate schemata and use critical thinking skills. Therefore, each book in the series promotes critical thinking skills before, during, and after the readings. The critical thinking skills include annotating a text, analyzing graphics, making inferences, and identifying fact and opinion. The readings encompass a wide range of academic disciplines: critical thinking, business, film studies, human geography, and biology. Chapters recycle reading skills (such as using titles, headings, and captions to predict) taught in previous chapters. Thus, students not only have opportunities to practice skills when they are taught, but they are given additional practice in later chapters using new academic content. Students are also able to self-monitor their reading speed by filling in a chart of timed readings. Intrinsically interesting content keeps students' attention as they develop their vocabulary and reading power.

Organization of the Book

Reading for a Reason 3 is a high-intermediate level book that prepares students for the academic reading they will have to do once they begin their academic coursework. *Reading for a Reason 3* features five units that span a variety of academic disciplines. Each unit begins with an introduction to the academic discipline including a definition and explanation, a list of important people in the field, and key questions to help students discover if they are attracted to the discipline. Each unit then consists of two 22-page chapters that integrate reading content with reading, vocabulary, speaking, writing, and Internet skills.

Each chapter has the following components:

▶ **What do you think?** promotes interactive pair work that personalizes the chapter topic.

▶ **Before You Read** stimulates background knowledge, focuses on vocabulary presentation and practice, and introduces important expressions.

▶ **Reading 1** introduces the chapter topic in a short informal reading. Types of texts include emails, film reviews, and newspaper and magazine articles.

▶ **Reading 2** introduces a longer, academic, scientific, or formal reading on the chapter topic.

▶ **Timed Reading** helps students become aware of and improve their reading speed by timing themselves and charting their times on the Timed Reading Chart in the back of the book.

▶ **Reading Skills** presents and has students practice reading comprehension skills needed to succeed in an academic environment.

▶ **After You Read** includes extended vocabulary practice, reading skills presentation and practice, as well as practice with collocations.

▶ **Talk About It** permits group discussions to help students synthesize, personalize, and extend concepts in the reading.

▶ **Expressions** presents collocations from Reading 1 and Reading 2. Practice exercises follow each presentation.

▶ **Internet Research** presents helpful tips on how to conduct academic research on the Internet. Practice exercises follow each presentation.

▶ **Write About It** provides opportunities for students to write at least two different paragraphs on ideas related to aspects of the chapter topic.

▶ **On Your Own** presents structured speaking activities that help students further explore each chapter theme.

▶ **Wrap Up** is an informal assessment tool that reviews chapter content, collocations, and reading skills.

▶ **Crossword Puzzle** reviews vocabulary taught in the chapter.

Audio Program

Each *Reading for a Reason* student book is paired with an audio program available on both audio CD and audiocassette. The audio program allows students to listen to the 20 reading passages as they read. Research shows that students learn in many ways. By allowing students aural input, the audio program strengthens the skill set of auditory learners. The audio program also facilitates pronunciation of individual words as well as the stress, intonation, and other suprasegmentals associated with collocations. Studies have also shown that listening to readings can help increase reading speed.

Teacher's Manuals

Each book in the series also has a Teacher's Manual that contains a complete answer key to the student book and chapter quizzes. The chapter quizzes consist of an additional reading passage on the chapter topic, five preview questions, five comprehension questions that reinforce the reading skills taught within the chapter, and five vocabulary questions. Quizzes can be photocopied and given to students for either review or assessment.

Think About Your Reading Skills

Think about your reading skills. Read the following statements and check the words that best describe you.

Before I begin a reading passage, I . . .	Never	Sometimes	Always
think about my personal connection to the topic.	_____	_____	_____
ask myself questions about the title.	_____	_____	_____
read the headings and subheadings.	_____	_____	_____
look at photos, charts, or tables and read their captions.	_____	_____	_____
read and think about the introduction.	_____	_____	_____
read the topic sentences of all the paragraphs.	_____	_____	_____

As I read a passage, I . . .	Never	Sometimes	Always
identify the main idea.	_____	_____	_____
identify details.	_____	_____	_____
identify examples.	_____	_____	_____
identify facts and opinions.	_____	_____	_____
take notes in the margin.	_____	_____	_____
guess the meanings of new words by using the context (the surrounding words) of each one.	_____	_____	_____

After I read a passage, I . . .	Never	Sometimes	Always
make a summary of what I read.	_____	_____	_____
predict questions about it that might be on a test.	_____	_____	_____
read it again.	_____	_____	_____

Skilled readers try to use the reading skills above as much as possible. If you don't, try to practice these skills **before, as,** and **after** you read.

UNIT 1 Critical Thinking

What is Critical Thinking?

Critical thinking is thinking intelligently about the world. Critical thinkers analyze ideas, exploring both positive and negative aspects of an idea or theory. They have open minds, make judgments by considering all sides of an issue, and are prepared to change their minds and rethink concepts, if necessary. Critical thinking involves:

- looking at evidence with an open mind
- evaluating theories, research, and ideas
- looking for weaknesses in one's own reasoning
- assessing the expertise of a writer or speaker
- looking for more than one expert who supports an idea
- asking questions to evaluate ideas

SOME FAMOUS CRITICAL THINKERS

Some famous people whose critical thinking ability is well respected include:

Lao Tse—Chinese philosopher, 570–490 B.C.

Plato—Greek philosopher, 427c–347 B.C.

Johannes Kepler—German mathematician and astronomer, 1571–1630

Abraham Lincoln—American president, 1809–1865

Winston Churchill—British statesman, 1874–1965

Susan Sontag—American writer, 1933–2004

Wangari Maathai—Kenyan human rights and environmental activist, 2004 Nobel Peace Prize winner, 1940–

Critical Thinking and You

If you are a successful critical thinker, you can go into any field that interests you, such as accounting, computer science, engineering, journalism, medicine, space exploration, teaching, law, or business.

Do you want a job that involves critical thinking? Ask yourself these questions:

- Do I think logically?
- Do I think independently?
- Do I enjoy evaluating new ideas, theories, and concepts?
- Am I willing to look at the weaknesses in my ideas as well as the strengths?

Introduction to Critical Thinking

CHAPTER PREVIEW

In this chapter, you'll:

Content
▶ read emails between students about the critical thinking courses they are taking
▶ discover barriers to critical thinking

Reading Skills
▶ prepare yourself physically and mentally for reading
▶ identify the main idea and supporting details of a reading

Vocabulary Skills
▶ use words and expressions for discussing critical thinking skills
▶ use collocations for describing critical thinking skills

Writing Skills
▶ describe a time you did or did not use critical thinking

Internet Skills
▶ do an effective Internet search using keywords

> What is the hardest task in the world? To think. 🕊
>
> — *Ralph Waldo Emerson*
> *(American Essayist, 1803–1882)*

SHORT SURVEY

I have an open mind when I:
- ❏ advise my friends
- ❏ read ads
- ❏ listen to political arguments
- ❏ read textbooks
- ❏ read newspapers
- ❏ advise myself
- ❏ other: _____

Reading 1:
What do two students think about their critical thinking courses? Read their emails to find out.

Reading 2:
What keeps people from thinking critically? "Barriers to Critical Thinking" has the answer.

What do you think?

Critical thinking is the ability to look at ideas objectively. Critical thinking helps people solve problems and make good decisions. Read each statement in the box below and decide if it's true or false. Circle your choice. Then discuss your answers with a partner.

Critical Thinking: What I Already Know

1. Only smart people find critical thinking easy.	True	False
2. Only well-educated people find critical thinking easy.	True	False
3. Thinking about your own interests can prevent critical thinking.	True	False
4. Critical thinkers can put themselves in another person's place.	True	False
5. Critical thinkers are self-centered.	True	False
6. You must be a good critical thinker to be a business manager.	True	False
7. Thinking that one's own country or culture is the best can prevent critical thinking.	True	False
8. People who are critical of others are critical thinkers.	True	False
9. Employers like to hire critical thinkers.	True	False
10. Using critical thinking can help you overcome prejudice.	True	False

Reading 1: A Critical Thinking Class

Before You Read

Preview

A. Reading 1 is an email exchange between friends. The title is "A Critical Thinking Class." What might the friends be talking about in their emails? Discuss your ideas with a partner.

B. What things are important to you when you decide to take a class? Read the items in the box below and circle your answers. Compare and discuss your answers with a partner.

1 = very important	2 = somewhat important	3 = not important at all		
1. The instructor is well-organized.		1	2	3
2. The instructor connects to me as a person.		1	2	3
3. The course content is connected to my everyday life.		1	2	3
4. The instructor has a good sense of humor.		1	2	3
5. The instructor gives a lot of tests.		1	2	3
6. The instructor gives few tests.		1	2	3
7. I have friends in the class.		1	2	3
8. The instructor gives interesting lectures.		1	2	3
9. The instructor gives personal opinions.		1	2	3
10. The information will be useful in my work.		1	2	3

C. Now discuss the following question: What else do you consider when you decide to take a class?

What else do you consider . . . ?

I . . .

Vocabulary

Here are some words from "A Critical Thinking Class." Complete each sentence with the correct word from the oval.

> covering   ~~drop~~   elements   relate   section   upcoming

1. "I hope this class isn't too difficult," said Marcy. "I know I can _____*drop*_____ it, but I would like to finish it."

2. Sam is running for president of the student association. The election is in two weeks, so he is working hard to win the _____ election.

3. There's a lot to learn in this course. Professor Thomas is _____ a lot of material.

4. The professor briefly introduced all the points about critical thinking that he wanted to cover on the first day. He said, "There are a lot of _____ to critical thinking, and we will cover many of them in this course."

5. "When the teacher talks about our lives, I can connect with the material. What I mean is I can _____ it to my own life," said Kevin.

6. "That critical thinking class is offered twice this term," said Paul. "One _____ meets on Mondays and Wednesdays. The other meets on Tuesdays and Thursdays."

As you read, think about this question:

▶ What is similar and different in Grace's and Roberto's critical thinking courses?

🎧 A Critical Thinking Class

Grace and Roberto are friends. They met in first grade. They lived near each other and they went to the same schools for 15 years. Now they go to the same college and are both taking a critical thinking course, but they're in different sections and have different professors. It's the second week of classes, and they are emailing
5 each other about their professors and courses.

#1

> **From:** Roberto Vasquez <rvasquez@bccc.cc.ca.us>
> **Date:** Thursday September 29, 2008 9:35 p.m.
> **To:** Grace Yee <gyee@bccc.cc.ca.us>
> **Subject:** How's your CT class going?
>
> 10   Hi Grace,
>
> How's your critical thinking class going? Mine's good. I think Professor Berman is great. She's really well-organized. She tries to relate what we're learning to our everyday lives. She's got a good sense of humor, too. How's Taylor's class and what are you guys covering?
>
> 15   -R.

From: Grace Yee <gyee@bccc.cc.ca.us>
Date: Thursday September 29, 2008 9:45 p.m.
To: Roberto Vasquez <rvasquez@bccc.cc.ca.us>
Subject: Re: How's your CT class going?

Hi Roberto,

Taylor's good, too. His syllabus looks great. We've got four tests, and he drops the lowest grade. Yay!!! I think that this stuff will be hard, but in the end, I know I'll be glad I took it. He started out talking about what critical thinking is. His introductory lecture was great. He talked about the elements of critical thinking.

The first thing he did was define it. He started with the word "critical" and talked about the two meanings of the word. The first meaning was negative, like when you try to figure out what's wrong with something, you find fault with it. (Remember we did that a lot when we were in high school and our parents couldn't do anything right!) The second meaning was more positive, about using good judgment and making good observations—in other words, thinking clearly and intelligently.

Jen just came in my room—more later.

Grace

#2

From: Roberto Vasquez <rvasquez@bccc.cc.ca.us>
Date: Thursday September 29, 2008 9:55 p.m.
To: Grace Yee <gyee@bccc.cc.ca.us>
Subject: Berman's class

Hi Grace,

Yeah, Berman started out with the same thing, a definition of critical thinking. She said we're going to learn to identify, analyze, and evaluate arguments and claims about the truth. She said we're going to learn to overcome personal prejudices and to make convincing arguments to support our ideas. This sounds good to me because I know it will help my writing . . .

She said she and the other professors don't really care so much about *what* we believe. They care more about *why* we believe it. That surprised me. Then she explained that in our courses the professors are looking at how we evaluate ideas and information. It's true, I think. Remember last semester in our biology class, Professor Miller gave us that question, "What would happen to the plant if . . . " and he didn't care if we said the plant would grow better or the plant would die as long as we had a good argument. He said the experiment hadn't been done and as long as we used what we had learned in the class and made a good argument, we would get full credit. I thought that was pretty cool.

Gotta get the phone. I'll get back to you, R.

#3

From: Grace Yee <gyee@bccc.cc.ca.us>
Date: Thursday September 29, 2008 10:30 p.m.
To: Roberto Vasquez <rvasquez@bccc.cc.ca.us>
Subject: Re: Berman's class

#4

Hey Roberto,

So, Jen said she's taking CT, too. We talked about maybe having a study group. What do you think?

Taylor also talked about how the course will help us in school, and he said that it'll also help us on the job. He said most employers want to hire people with critical thinking skills. He said employers say that what they really need are quick learners and people who can solve problems, think creatively, gather and analyze information, and draw appropriate conclusions from data. Also, they want people who communicate their ideas clearly and effectively. He said courses in critical thinking help people do that. I think we're doing the right thing by taking it this fall.

So what do you say—we're all using the same book, so do you want to be in a study group with Jen and me? Our first test is in two weeks. ☺

Grace

From: Roberto Vasquez <rvasquez@bccc.cc.ca.us>
Date: Thursday September 29, 2008 10:45 p.m.
To: Grace Yee <gyee@bccc.cc.ca.us>
Subject: Study group

#5

Hi Grace,

Yes, let's make a study group. We've got a test in a couple of weeks, too. She said she'd focus the first test on critical thinking in daily life. So I think she may use arguments from the candidates in the upcoming election, or ads from TV, magazines, and the Internet.

Fridays at 3:00 work for me. You? Jen?

-R.

85

From: Grace Yee <gyee@bccc.cc.ca.us>
Date: Thursday September 29, 2008 11:00 p.m.
To: Roberto Vasquez <rvasquez@bccc.cc.ca.us>
Subject: Re: Study group

Hi Roberto,

Great! Fridays work for me, too. I'll ask Jen.

90

See you in the student lounge at 3:00. We can figure out where to go from there.

Grace

Word Count: 851 words

Timed Reading

Read "A Critical Thinking Class" again. Read at a comfortable speed. Time your reading. You will read it again later and time yourself again. Write your time in the Timed Reading Chart on page 232.

Start time: _____ *(11:00)*

End time: _____ *(11:15)*

My reading time: _____ *(15 minutes)*

Students usually have to read a lot. In each chapter, you will be asked to do four timed readings. These timed readings will help you increase your reading speed.

After You Read

Comprehension

1. Write a statement that describes the main idea of the emails between Grace and Roberto.

   _____

   _____

2. Explain Grace's attitude toward Professor Taylor's course. Include a detail from her email that

   supports your explanation. _____

   _____

3. Explain why Roberto thinks that Professor Berman is a good professor. Include an example

   from Roberto's email that supports your explanation. _____

   _____

4. Explain in your own words Professor Taylor's two meanings of "critical." _____

   _____

5. According to Grace, what does Professor Taylor say that employers want? _____

   _____

6. What do Grace and Roberto think will be the benefit of a study group? _____

   _____

Talk About It

Discuss these questions.
1. Do you study in a group? Why or why not?
2. Have you taken a critical thinking class? If so, what did you learn?

Reading 2: Barriers to Critical Thinking

Before You Read

Preview

A. The title of Reading 2 is "Barriers to Critical Thinking." What do you think might make it difficult to think critically? Try to give an example. Discuss your ideas with a partner.

B. Preview these words and expressions from the reading. Complete each sentence with the correct word or expression.

barrier	conformism	outgrow	trait
bias	herd instinct	tendency	unwarranted

1. People have many characteristics that help them succeed. One _____ may be the ability to stay with a project until it is completed.

2. People sometimes have a(n) _____. This means like some animals, they naturally travel together in groups.

3. _____—the need to follow the group—is typical of teenagers. For example, 16-year-old Dan and his friends wear the same style of clothes and listen to the same type of music.

4. By the time Dan is 20, he will probably _____ the need to dress just like his friends.

5. Professors should never show a(n) _____ towards a student. It would be unfair to show they like one student more than the others.

6. Victor has a(n) _____ to make decisions quickly. Sometimes he decides too fast and then later regrets his decision.

7. Often it is difficult to find out what the _____ is that keeps us from making a change in our life. We want to make the change, but find it too hard.

8. I came to a(n) _____ conclusion in my paper on cloning because I didn't take the time to research all the facts and the history.

Reading Skills

Getting Ready to Read

Good readers prepare themselves both physically and mentally for reading. Here are some ways to get ready to read.

Physical Preparation: To prepare physically, make sure that you are sitting in a comfortable chair. If you're reading a textbook and need to take notes, sit at a desk. Make sure you have good light. The light should be behind you and to the side. Your head shouldn't make a shadow on the page. Read in a quiet place unless you can "tune out" (disregard) noise and like to read in a café, coffee shop, or the student union. Take a break from your reading about every 45 minutes.

Mental Preparation: Mental preparation is also important, especially if you have a lot of reading to do. Think about why you are doing the reading. Ask yourself, "Why am I reading this? What do I want to know when I am finished?" Be positive. For example, tell yourself: "I will accomplish my reading goals, and I will know what I want to know when I am finished." If you are having trouble understanding your reading, take a break and do something else. Talk to a friend, play a game, or go for a walk. Go back to the hard parts and reread them later.

Practice

Analyze your reading habits. Fill in the following chart with different types of reading materials. Then compare your answers with your classmates' answers.

What I Read	Where I Read	Conditions	Comments
Newspapers	Student Union	Good lighting; lots of noise; easy to get coffee	Fine for newspaper reading; not good for textbooks

As you read, think about this question:
▶ How can you be a critical thinker?

🎧 Barriers to Critical Thinking

Critical thinking helps people solve problems and make good decisions. Uncritical thinking is common. Many people, including smart and well-educated people, find critical thinking difficult. Here is a list of some of the most common barriers to critical thinking:

5
- egocentrism (self-centered thinking)
- face-saving
- lack of relevant background information
- overpowering emotions
- self-deception
10
- self-interested thinking
- sociocentrism (group-centered thinking)
- superstition
- unwarranted assumptions

The Thinker, *Auguste Rodin*

Three of these—egocentrism, sociocentrism, and
15 unwarranted assumptions—play an especially powerful role in preventing critical thinking. Let's look at these one at a time.

Egocentrism

Egocentrism is the tendency to see reality as centered on oneself. Egocentrics are selfish people who feel that their own interests, ideas, and values are better
20 than other people's. Do you know people like that?

There are many kinds of egocentrism. Two kinds of egocentrism are self-interested thinking and self-serving bias. Everyone uses self-interested thinking some of the time. For example, students may want the library open until 2:00 A.M., but the administration wants to save money and close the library at 11:00 P.M. The
25 librarians don't want to work late at night. They want the library to close at 9 P.M. Critical thinking shows us that we shouldn't say, "This benefits me, so it must be good." We have to look at all the evidence and arguments objectively to see what is best for the majority of the people who are affected by the situation.

Self-serving bias is the tendency to overrate oneself—to see oneself as being
better in some way than one actually is. We all know people who claim to be more
talented or knowledgeable than they actually are. Studies show that self-serving
bias is an extremely common psychological trait. In one survey, one million high
school seniors were asked to rate themselves on their "ability to get along with
others." Not a single person marked him- or herself "below average" on this trait.
Other surveys show that 90 percent of business managers and 90 percent of college professors rate themselves as "better than average" on their performance. Of
course, no one likes to think, "I am below average." And of course, each person
is below average in some way. We want to set high goals for ourselves, but if we
are overconfident, then we may not grow personally or intellectually.

Sociocentrism

A second barrier to critical thinking is sociocentrism. This is group-centered
thinking. Two kinds of sociocentrism are group bias and herd instinct (or conformism). Group bias is the tendency to see one's own group as being better than
others. The group could be a nation, a peer group, a family, or any other social
group. Thinking "my group is the best" has been very common throughout
human history and across cultures. We find it easy to hold a high view of our family, our community, or our nation. It is also easy to look down on people we think
are "outsiders."

We get our group bias unconsciously, usually in early childhood. There is a
story of an eight-year-old Swiss boy who thought that being Swiss was the best.
He said that he thought a French boy would believe that being French was best,
but the French boy would be wrong. "Why would the French boy be wrong?"
someone asked the Swiss boy. The Swiss boy said that the French boy would
be wrong because being Swiss was best. We usually outgrow the idea that our
country is best at everything. Then, we say how other countries may be better in
some things, but we usually also give reasons why our country is the best in other
things.

The second kind of sociocentrism is herd instinct (or conformism). Herd instinct
refers to the tendency to follow the crowd. It is the tendency to conform to authority or to the group standard of conduct or belief without thinking. The desire to
belong, to be part of a group, is very strong in humans. No one likes to be left out.

Unwarranted Assumptions

A third barrier to critical thinking is unwarranted assumptions. An assumption is something we believe to be true without proof. Most things we think and
do are based on assumptions. We have assumptions about how long it will take us

to get to class or to work. We have assumptions about the weather. If the weather report says that it will rain, we take an umbrella because we assume that the weatherman is not lying and that the weather report is based on scientific evidence. There may be no proof that it will rain, but we realize that we don't have time to
70 do the research necessary to prove that the weatherman is wrong, and that the weather report is based on scientific evidence, so we just take an umbrella. Taking an umbrella usually does not lead to problems, but sometimes we are unhappy when we make an assumption that has no basis in fact. Sometimes, because we like someone very much, we make the
75 assumption that the other person likes us, too. When we find out our assumption is wrong, we become very sad. A good rule is not to make assumptions without enough information.

An unwarranted assumption is an unreasonable assumption. Stereotypes are unwarranted assumptions. A stereotype
80 is an oversimplified mental picture of an individual or group of people. If you meet a South Bergian (not a real group of people) who is cruel and rude, and you say all South Bergians are cruel and rude, you are stereotyping South Bergians. If you have an opinion of a person based on the group the per-
85 son belongs to, and you don't look at that person as an individual, you are stereotyping.

Yerakdu (The Thinker) by Simon Gambulo Marmos and Joe Mare Wakundi

There are many barriers to critical thinking. Egocentrism, sociocentrism, and unwarranted assumptions are a few of them. If you know about these barriers, it can help you be a better thinker. This, in turn, can help
90 you at school, at work, and when making decisions in daily life.

Word Count: 994

Source: *Critical Thinking: A Student's Introduction* (Bassham, et al.)

Timed Reading

Read "Barriers to Critical Thinking" again. Read at a comfortable speed. Time your reading. Write your time in the Timed Reading Chart on page 232.

Start time: _____

End time: _____

My reading time: _____

I was never as good as all the credit I got and never as bad as the criticism I received. 🔔

— *Roger Smith (American CEO of General Motors, b. 1925)*

Reading Skills

Identifying the Main Idea and Supporting Ideas

When you read, it's important to get the main idea of a passage. The main idea is the writer's general message. Usually, there is a main idea to the whole reading. Major sections of a reading may each have a main idea, as well. Individual paragraphs in the reading may also each have a main idea. These ideas are called "supporting ideas" because they support the main idea of the whole reading.

Authors often state the main idea of a reading in the introduction—but not always. Main ideas of paragraphs and sections can be at the beginning, in the middle, or at the end. If you can't find the main idea, ask yourself, "What is the author's main point? Why did he or she write this?"

After you find the main idea, look for the supporting ideas. There are usually examples. Once you understand the main idea and supporting ideas, you understand the reading.

Practice

Find a sentence in "Barriers to Critical Thinking" that states the main idea and underline it. Then answer these questions.

1. Where in the reading did you find it? _____

   _____

2. Where are the supporting ideas found in the reading? _____

   _____

   _____

3. Write in your own words a statement that describes the main idea of "Barriers to Critical Thinking."

   _____

   _____

   _____

Getting the Details

A. Answer the following questions. Use complete sentences.

1. Explain in your own words the term *self-serving bias* and give an example.

   _____

   _____

2. Explain what the story about the Swiss boy illustrates.

   _____

   _____

3. Explain in your own words what *herd instinct* means and give an example.

   _____

   _____

4. According to the authors, where do we get our group bias?

   _____

   _____

5. Why do the authors say that unwarranted assumptions are a barrier to critical thinking?

   _____

   _____

B. Fill in the following chart. Write a definition and an example of each of the terms.

Concept	Definition	Example
Egocentricism		
Sociocentrism		
Unwarranted Assumptions		

Vocabulary

A. Here are some more words from "Barriers to Critical Thinking." Find them in the reading and circle them.

Nouns	Verb	Adjective	Adverbs
authority	overrate	unreasonable	objectively
stereotype			unconsciously

B. Now use them to complete the sentences.

1. People who say "All North Bergians are sweet and kind" have a(n) _____ of North Bergians.

2. If you don't think about your decisions and you make them _____, you can end up making poor decisions.

3. My friend told me not to _____ myself. She said people who have too high an opinion of themselves are often unhappy.

4. If you don't have good reasons for a decision, you may make a(n) _____ one that you will regret later.

5. Your boss, supervisor, or other people in _____ have the right to tell you what to do at work, but they still want you to think critically.

6. It's good to examine all the facts _____ before you form an opinion. Then you will have a less biased opinion.

Talk About It

Discuss these questions.

1. Describe situations when you or someone you know experienced egocentrism and sociocentrism.
2. Describe a time when you made an unwarranted assumption. What was the situation? What happened? What was the consequence?

Expressions

Collocations for Discussing Critical Thinking

Collocations are words that are frequently used together. For example, during a meal, your friend may say, "Salt and pepper, please." In fact, it would sound strange if your friend were to say, "Pepper and salt, please." This is because "salt and pepper" is a collocation. Native speakers expect to see or hear those words in a certain order.

Here are some collocations for the two readings in this chapter. They relate to critical thinking issues. Notice that some are verb phrases (they act like verbs in a sentence) and some are noun phrases (they act like nouns). Collocations can also work like adverbs and adjectives. It's important to pay attention to how collocations fit in a sentence.

be exercising good judgment (verb phrase)
convincing arguments (noun phrase)
draw appropriate conclusions (verb phrase)
find fault (verb phrase)
personal prejudices (noun phrase)

Example:
I don't think that Roger had very **convincing arguments**. I still think he was wrong.

Practice

A. Find and underline the collocations in the box above in "A Critical Thinking Class" and "Barriers to Critical Thinking."

B. Now use some of them to complete the sentences.

1. _____ keep people from "seeing the big picture" and from understanding someone else's point of view.

2. People who always _____ with others are not fun to be around, and often find themselves left out because they are so critical.

3. John said, "I think arguing with people is fun because I can present

   _____ and persuade people to take my side."

4. Think carefully when you analyze a problem. Then you will be able to

   _____ and solve the problem. By not coming to a quick

   conclusion you will _____ .

Internet Research

Doing an Effective Search

When you use a search engine such as Google.com (**www.google.com**) to do a keyword search, using the right keywords saves you time. Keywords should not be too general. Also, you can often combine keywords to get exactly what you want. In addition, combining keywords can help you get fewer results. For example, if you wanted books on critical thinking for college students you could type: *critical thinking books college students*. Note: You don't need words such as *on* and *for*.

To limit a search even more, put quotation marks around your keywords. For example, if you search for *critical thinking,* you can get over 5,600,000 results. If you do a search for *"critical thinking,"* you will have a lot fewer results.

Practice

Practice combining keywords and using quotation marks. Try looking for the following:

- ▶ research on critical thinking
- ▶ research on college students and critical thinking
- ▶ courses in critical thinking
- ▶ creativity, egocentrism, and critical thinking
- ▶ (your choice)

Take notes on the keyword combinations you used and whether or not you used quotation marks. Which gave you the most useful search results? Discuss your experience with the class.

Write About It

Write about critical thinking. Choose one of these topics:

- ▶ Write about a time when you did or did not use critical thinking. Describe the situation and your thought process.
- ▶ Describe your favorite place to read. What makes it your favorite place? What do you like to read there? Do you only read there or do you do other things? If you do other things, what are they? Do they distract you or help you read?

Use five words and expressions from this chapter. Also, try to use your Internet research.

On Your Own

Project

Take a survey. Ask your classmates about unwarranted assumptions they've made about a new country, city, or other place they visited. That is, what ideas did they have about the place before they went? How did their ideas change after the visit?

Step 1: Prepare

Listen as your teacher reads the survey questions in the box below. Do you understand them? Repeat the questions with your teacher so you can pronounce them correctly.

Step 2: Take a Survey

Ask three classmates about their experience with unwarranted assumptions. Fill in the box below.

Unwarranted Assumptions Survey

1. What place did you visit?

Person 1: _____

Person 2: _____

Person 3: _____

2. What unwarranted assumptions did you have?

Person 1: _____

Person 2: _____

Person 3: _____

3. What did you find instead?

Person 1: _____

Person 2: _____

Person 3: _____

Step 3: Follow-Up

Discuss the results of your survey with the class. For example, you might discuss if there is a pattern in people's assumptions about a new place.

Wrap Up

How Much Do You Remember?

Check your new knowledge. In this chapter you learned facts, words, and expressions. You also learned reading skills and you practiced writing. Complete the following to check what you remember.

1. What are two meanings of the word *critical*? _____

   _____

2. How is critical thinking useful in daily life? _____

   _____

3. What are two kinds of *egocentrism*? _____

   _____

4. What are two kinds of *sociocentrism*? _____

   _____

5. Use *objectively* in a sentence. _____

   _____

6. What are some ways to prepare for reading? _____

   _____

   _____

7. How can you limit an Internet search? _____

   _____

   _____

Second Timed Readings

Now reread "A Critical Thinking Class" and "Barriers to Critical Thinking." Time each reading separately. Write your times in the Timed Reading Chart on page 232.

Crossword Puzzle

Complete the crossword puzzle to practice some words and expressions from this chapter.

CLUES

Across ➔
2. Prejudice
3. No longer need due to maturity
6. Doing the same as others do
9. A person in power
10. A belief that all people in a group share the same characteristics
11. Without being thoughtful

Down ↓
1. Good, strong arguments
2. Another word for *obstacle*
4. Without reason
5. Criticize
7. Doing something in a way that is without prejudice
8. Rate too highly

CHAPTER 2

Problem Solving

CHAPTER PREVIEW

In this chapter, you'll:

Content
- ▶ read about how to prepare for problem solving
- ▶ learn strategies for solving problems creatively

Reading Skills
- ▶ preview a reading by reviewing the title and headings
- ▶ learn two ways to take notes on a reading

Vocabulary Skills
- ▶ use words and expressions for talking about critical thinking and problem solving
- ▶ use collocations for discussing creative problem solving

Writing Skills
- ▶ describe a difficult problem to solve and explain why it's so difficult
- ▶ describe a problem that you solved and explain how you solved it

Internet Skills
- ▶ evaluate URLs in Internet search results

> To ask the right question is already half the solution to a problem. ❧
>
> — *Carl G. Jung*
> *(Swiss psychiatrist, 1875–1961)*

SHORT SURVEY

In my opinion, the most difficult problems to solve are:
- ❑ math problems
- ❑ personal problems
- ❑ school or work problems
- ❑ relationship problems
- ❑ world problems
- ❑ other: _____

Reading 1:
What should you do when you have a problem to solve? Read "Preparing Your Mind for Problem Solving" to find out.

Reading 2:
How easy is it to become a creative problem solver? Find out in "Creative Problem Solving."

Complete the sentences in the box below.
Then compare your answers with a partner.

My Problem-Solving Style

1. I usually find it _____ to solve problems.

_____ easy   _____ difficult

2. When I have a family problem to solve, I usually feel _____.

_____ excited   _____ anxious   _____ neutral (neither excited nor anxious)

3. When I have a school problem to solve, I usually feel _____.

_____ excited   _____ anxious   _____ neutral (neither excited nor anxious)

4. When I have to help a friend solve a problem, I usually feel _____.

_____ excited   _____ anxious   _____ neutral (neither excited nor anxious)

5. I like to do math problems.

_____ Yes   _____ No

6. I like word games (crossword puzzles, jumbles, Scrabble).

_____ Yes   _____ No

7. When I have a difficult problem, I usually _____.

_____ try to forget about it   _____ start trying to solve it immediately

8. I feel that _____.

_____ I am a good problem solver   _____ I need to improve my problem-solving skills

Reading 1: Preparing Your Mind for Problem Solving

Before You Read

Preview

A. The title of Reading 1 is "Preparing Your Mind for Problem Solving." What kind of information might it include? Discuss your ideas with a partner.

> Clinging to the past is the problem. Embracing change is the answer. ❧
>
> — *Gloria Steinem*
> *(American journalist, b. 1934)*

B. How do you approach a difficult problem? Circle *Agree* or *Disagree* for each statement. Compare and discuss your answers with a partner.

1. When I have a difficult problem to solve, I usually have a positive attitude.

   Agree   Disagree

2. I try to avoid dealing with problems.

   Agree   Disagree

3. I don't use any special strategies when solving problems or making decisions.

   Agree   Disagree

4. When making a decision, I try to use critical thinking skills.

   Agree   Disagree

5. I usually stick with my first decision when solving problems.

   Agree   Disagree

6. If I have a difficult problem to solve, I usually give up pretty quickly.

   Agree   Disagree

7. When solving problems, I usually ask for help.

   Agree   Disagree

Vocabulary

Here are some words and expressions from "Preparing Your Mind for Problem Solving." Match them with the highlighted words or expressions in the sentences. Write the letter of the correct answer on the line.

> a. assess   c. decoding   e. is fundamental to   g. perceive
> b. criteria   d. inquisitive   f. multidimensional   h. sustained

__e__ **1.** Thinking critically **is a basic part of** creative problem solving.

_____ **2.** Creative problem solving is **complex**. It isn't a simple process at all.

_____ **3.** If you **think of** problems as games, they are often easier to solve.

_____ **4.** A good critical thinker can **evaluate** other people's statements without judging them.

_____ **5.** Solving problems effectively requires a **continuous** effort. You can't give up too soon.

_____ **6.** Being **curious** is a characteristic of good critical thinkers.

_____ **7.** During World War II, the Germans developed the Enigma Machine, a machine that created codes for sending secret messages. However, Allied code breakers were capable of **deciphering** many of the messages that the machine generated.

_____ **8.** Good critical thinkers are able to analyze ideas based on a clearly defined set of **conditions**.

The Enigma Machine

As you read, think about this question:

▶ What three strategies can help you prepare for problem solving?

🎧 Preparing Your Mind for Problem Solving

All problem solving—whether personal or academic—involves decision-making. You have to make decisions to solve the problem. However, some problems occur because of the decisions you
5   have made. In your school life, you may decide not to study mathematics and science because you consider them too hard. Because of this decision, certain careers will be closed to you. You can see that many events in your life do not just happen; they are the result of your choices and decisions.
10   Critical thinking and creativity can help you solve both personal and academic problems.

The following three strategies, based on a logical and scientific approach to problem solving, may help when you face a decision or try to solve a problem:

1. Have a positive attitude. Your attitude has a lot to do with how you
15   approach and solve a problem or make a decision. Look at all problems as opportunities. For example, if you think science and math courses are difficult, approach these courses with a positive and inquisitive attitude. Think of problems as puzzles to solve rather than homework to avoid.

2. Use critical thinking. Critical thinking helps you find the best solution. It is
20   a multidimensional process that involves decoding, analyzing, processing, reasoning, and evaluating information. It is also an attitude: a willingness and a passion to explore, probe, question, and search for answers and solutions. (See "Attributes of a Critical Thinker," on page 31). Critical thinking is fundamental to problem solving.

25   **3. Persistence pays off.** Coming to a solution requires sustained effort. You can't give up and a problem may not always be solved with your first effort. Sometimes a second or third try will get you the results you need or want. Sometimes even more than that.

Attributes of a Critical Thinker

30   Critical thinkers have certain characteristics. Do these attributes describe you?

- They are willing to ask questions and assess statements and arguments.

35
- They have the ability to suspend judgment and tolerate ambiguity.

- They have the ability to admit a lack of information or understanding, and when they don't understand, they keep asking until they do.

40
- They have a curiosity and interest in seeking new solutions, and they aren't afraid of trying something new.

- They have the ability to clearly define a set of criteria for analyzing ideas.

- They have a willingness to examine beliefs, assumptions, and opinions against facts.

45   The good news is that anyone can become a critical thinker and use creativity to solve problems. Once you open your mind to new ways of seeing issues, you can enjoy solving problems of all types, both academic and personal.

Word Count: 488

Source: *Peak Performance: Success in College and Beyond* (Ferrett)

> I am not judged by the number of times I fail, but by the number of times I succeed; and the number of times I succeed is in direct proportion to the number of times I can fail and keep on trying. ❧
>
> — *Tom Hopkins*
> *(American entrepreneur)*

Timed Reading

Read "Preparing Your Mind for Problem Solving" again. Read at a comfortable speed. Time your reading. Write your time in the Timed Reading Chart on page 232.

Start time: _____

End time: _____

My reading time: _____

After You Read

Comprehension

1. Write a statement that expresses the main idea of "Preparing Your Mind for Problem Solving." _____

   _____

2. According to the author, why is it important to use creativity and critical thinking skills?

   _____

   _____

3. Give an example of having a positive attitude about problem solving. _____

   _____

4. Give an example of having a negative attitude about problem solving. _____

   _____

5. List some of the characteristics of good critical thinkers. _____

   _____

6. Explain in your own words why persistence enhances problem solving. _____

   _____

Talk About It

Discuss these questions.
1. Do you agree or disagree with the author's ideas about problem solving?
2. Think of a problem that you had to solve recently. How did you solve it? Did you have a positive attitude? Why or why not? Did you use critical thinking? If so, give an example. Were you persistent? Why or why not?

Do you agree or disagree with the author's ideas?

I . . .

Reading 2: Creative Problem Solving

Before You Read

Reading Skills

Previewing a Reading

Previewing a reading before you read it helps you read it faster and more efficiently. There are many ways to preview a textbook chapter. One is to read and think about the chapter title and the headings that divide the chapter into sections. The title often gives hints about the main idea, and the headings often tell you the supporting ideas. (Note: Titles and headings are usually **bolded** or in a larger size than the rest of the type. Sometimes they are lettered or numbered.)

Before you read, scan the title and the headings. Ask yourself questions about them. Then make guesses about the reading. For example, look at the title and heading for Reading 2 in Chapter 1 (page 15):

Title: "Barriers to Critical Thinking"

Questions: What are some barriers to critical thinking? How will identifying barriers make someone a better thinker?

Headings: Egocentrism, Sociocentrism, Unwarranted Assumptions

Questions: What are these barriers? How do they interfere with critical thinking?

Guesses about the reading: I think this reading describes behaviors or attitudes that make critical thinking more difficult. Some of these attitudes may be egocentrism, sociocentrism, and unwarranted assumptions. The reading probably explains why these behaviors are barriers to critical thinking and how to avoid them.

Practice

Preview the title and the headings in Reading 2 on pages 36–38. Fill in the box below. Work with a partner.

The title of Reading 2 is: _____

Questions about the title include: _____

_____

The headings for Reading 2 are:

1: _____   5: _____

2: _____   6: _____

3: _____   7: _____

4: _____

Questions about the headings include: _____

_____

_____

_____

Guesses about the reading: _____

_____

_____

_____

_____

_____

Preview

A. The title of Reading 2 is "Creative Problem Solving." You read a little about strategies for creative problem solving in Reading 1, and you previewed the headings for Reading 2. How might certain strategies help in solving problems? Discuss a few examples with a partner.

B. Preview these words from the reading. Decide if each statement below is *T* (True) or *F* (False). Circle T or F.

1. If you **abandon** something, it means you keep it forever.   T F

2. An **affirmation** is a positive statement.   T F

3. A **breakthrough** is an innovation or a new idea.   T F

4. **Mental blocks** are ideas that help your thoughts flow freely.   T F

5. A **nonconformist** is just like everyone else.   T F

6. To **putter** around the house is to do small tasks at home.   T F

7. To **strive to** do something is to work very hard for it.   T F

8. You are usually aware of your **subconscious** thoughts.   T F

C. Preview these idiomatic expressions from the reading. Match them with the words and expressions that mean about the same thing.

Idioms	Meanings
_____ 1. an "aha" experience	**a.** always be doing the same thing
_____ 2. be in a rut	**b.** a safe route
_____ 3. broke with tradition	**c.** do something without taking chances
_____ 4. no-risk path	**d.** things that help you reach a goal
_____ 5. play it safe	**e.** did something in a new way
_____ 6. stepping-stones	**f.** an experience that makes a person see something in a new way

As you read, think about this question:
▶ How can certain strategies make you a better problem solver?

Albert Einstein

🎧 Creative Problem Solving

Creativity is thinking of something different, using new approaches to solve problems. Many inventions have involved a breakthrough in traditional thinking and resulted in an "aha" experience. For example, Albert Einstein broke with tradition by trying many unusual approaches that revolutionized scientific 5 thought. Your attitudes can form mental blocks that keep you from being creative. If you find yourself imprisoned by routines, afraid to look foolish, and reluctant to challenge the rules or allow failure, you may be in a rut. Before long, you may abandon your dreams; ignore your intuition; deny problems; and follow a too-safe, no-risk path. Try the following seven strategies to unlock your 10 mind's natural creativity.

1. Use games and puzzles. Turn problems into puzzles to be solved. Rethinking an assignment as a puzzle, a challenge, or a game instead of a difficult problem allows an open frame of mind and encourages your creative side to operate. Creative people often get fresh ideas when they are having fun and are 15 involved in an unrelated activity. When your defenses are down, which means you are relaxed, your subconscious is alive and creative thoughts can flow.

2. Challenge the rules. Habit often restricts you from trying new approaches to problem solving. Often there is more than one solution. List many alternatives, choices, and solutions, and imagine the likely consequences of each. Empty 20 your mind of the "right" way of looking at a problem and strive to see situations in a fresh, new way. How many times have you told yourself that you must follow certain rules and perform tasks a certain way? If you want to be creative, try new approaches, look at things in a new order, break the pattern, and challenge the rules. Practice a different approach by completing the Nine-25 Dot Exercise in Figure 2.1.

Join all the dots with just four straight lines, without lifting the pen from the paper.

Figure 2.1: *Nine-Dot Exercise*

3. **Brainstorm.** Brainstorming is a common creative strategy that frees the imagination. With this strategy, a group thinks of as many ideas as possible. Brainstorming encourages the mind to explore new approaches without judging the merit of these ideas. In fact, even silly and irrelevant ideas can lead to truly inventive ideas. While brainstorming ideas for a speech, one study group started making jokes about the topic, and new ideas came from all directions. Humor can generate ideas, put you in a creative state of mind, and can make work fun. Top executives, scientists, doctors, and artists know that they can extend the boundaries of their knowledge by allowing themselves to extend their limits. They ask, "What if?"

4. **Work to change mind-sets.** It is difficult to see another frame of reference once your mind is set. Try the exercise in Figure 2.2. Do you see an old woman, a young woman, or both? This is an "aha" exercise. It is exciting to watch people really see the other picture. There is enormous power in shifting your perception and gaining new ways of seeing things, events, and people. Perceptual exercises of this kind clearly demonstrate that we see what we focus on. You are conditioned to see certain things, depending on your beliefs and attitudes. Rather than seeing facts, you may see your interpretation of reality. To solve problems effectively, you need to see objects and events objectively, not through perceptual filters.

Figure 2.2: *Old woman/young woman illusion*

5. **Change your routine.** Try a different route to work or school. At your favorite restaurant, order new dishes. Read different kinds of books. Become totally involved in a project. Stay in bed and read all day. Spend time with people who are different from you. In other words, occasionally break away from your daily routine and take time every day to relax, daydream, putter, and renew your energy. Look at unexpected events as an opportunity to retreat from

constant activity and hurried thoughts. Perhaps this is a good time to brainstorm ideas for a speech assignment or outline an assigned paper. Creative
ideas need time to develop.

6. **Allow failure.** Remember that if you don't fail occasionally, you are not risking
anything. Mistakes are stepping-stones to growth and creativity. Fear of failure
undermines the creative process by forcing us to play it safe. Eliminate the fear
and shame of failure that you experienced in earlier years and learn to admit
mistakes. Looking at your mistakes as stepping-stones and opportunities for
growth will allow this shift. Ask yourself: "What did I learn from this mistake?
How can I handle the same type of situation the next time? How can I prepare
for a situation like this the next time?" Creative people aren't afraid to look
foolish at times, to generate unusual ideas, and to be nonconformists. They
tend not to take themselves too seriously.

7. **Expect to be creative.** Everyone can be creative. To be a creative person, try to
see yourself as a creative person. Say affirmations that reinforce your innate
creativity:
 • I am a creative and resourceful person.
 • I have many imaginative and unusual ideas.
 • Creative ideas flow to me many times a day, and I act on these ideas.
 These seven strategies have worked for many people. Try them the next time
you have to solve a difficult problem.

Word Count: 947

Source: *Peak Performance: Success in College and Beyond* (Ferrett)

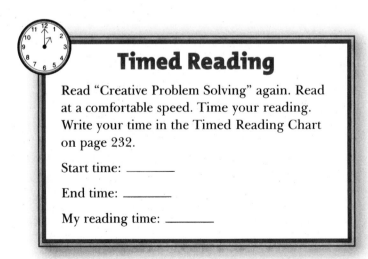

Timed Reading

Read "Creative Problem Solving" again. Read
at a comfortable speed. Time your reading.
Write your time in the Timed Reading Chart
on page 232.

Start time: _____

End time: _____

My reading time: _____

After You Read

Main Idea

Write a statement that expresses the main idea of "Creative Problem Solving."

_____

_____

_____

Getting the Details

Answer the following questions. Use complete sentences.

1. Why does the author suggest that you turn problems into puzzles?

_____

_____

2. What is the purpose of brainstorming, according to the author?

_____

_____

3. Express in your own words the author's attitude toward failure.

_____

_____

4. What is the exercise in Figure 2.1 an example of?

_____

_____

5. Give two examples of statements that are affirmations.

_____

_____

Taking Notes as You Read

Good readers take notes as they read. They make notes about the information in the reading that is relevant to their purpose. For example, if you are reading for an exam, you take notes on information that you think will prepare you for it. If you are writing a paper, you take notes on information that you will need to develop your ideas. Either way, taking notes helps you recognize the main and supporting ideas of a reading and helps you retain information better.

There are many ways to makes notes as you read. One way is to make an outline of the main and supporting ideas. Another is to create a graphic organizer. When you take notes, avoid using complete sentences. Paraphrase and use abbreviations whenever possible.

Here is an example of notes for "Preparing Your Mind for Problem Solving" on pages 30 and 31. Another example is on page 41.

Traditional Outline

I. Introduction/Main Idea: Using certain strategies can help you solve problems.

II. Three Strategies for Problem Solving
   A. Positive attitude
        Ex.: approach problems as puzzles
   B. Critical thinking
        Ex.: decode, analyze, evaluate, question, etc.
   C. Persistence
        Ex.: sometimes you need several tries

III. Attributes of a Critical Thinker
   A. Ask questions
   B. Suspend judgment & tolerate ambiguity
   C. Ask for help if you need it
   D. Don't be afraid of trying something new
   E. Have a system for analyzing ideas
   F. Be open-minded

(Continue)

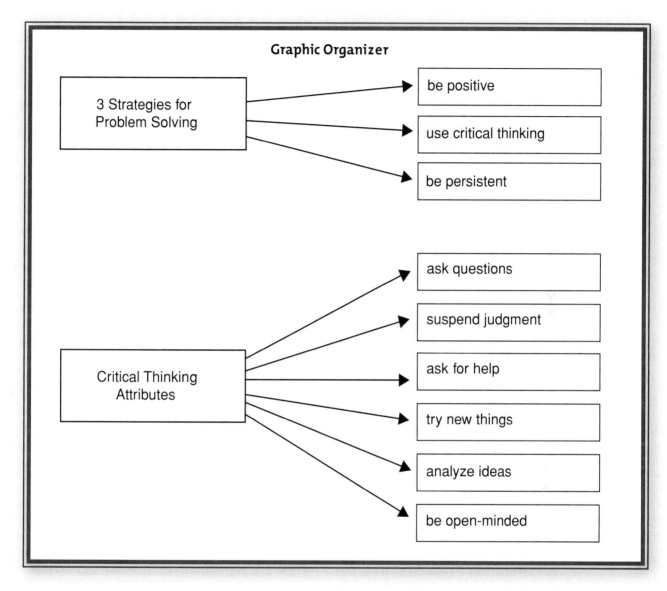

Graphic Organizer

3 Strategies for Problem Solving
- be positive
- use critical thinking
- be persistent

Critical Thinking Attributes
- ask questions
- suspend judgment
- ask for help
- try new things
- analyze ideas
- be open-minded

Practice

Re-read "Creative Problem Solving." On a separate piece of paper, take notes on the main and supporting ideas. Include important examples. Use either a traditional outline or a graphic organizer. Compare your notes with a partner's notes and discuss the following questions:

1. Which note-taking format did you use? Why?

2. In your opinion, are your partner's notes complete? What did you include that your partner did not? Why? What did your partner include that you did not? Why?

Vocabulary

A. Here are some more words and expressions from "Creative Problem Solving." Find them in the reading and circle them.

Nouns	Verbs	Adjective
a. an open frame of mind b. perceptual filters	c. imprisoned by d. take themselves too seriously	e. reluctant

B. Now match them with the highlighted words in the sentences. Write the letter of the correct answer on the line.

_____ **1.** James is **unwilling** to see things in a new way, so he's going to have a hard time solving his problems.

_____ **2.** Chris can't look at a situation clearly without **his beliefs and attitudes interfering with his thinking**.

_____ **3.** Conformists tend to **be afraid of looking foolish**.

_____ **4.** Linda felt **trapped by** her daily routine, so she decided to make some big changes in her life.

_____ **5.** It is good to look at things with **a relaxed mind**.

Talk About It

Discuss these questions.
1. How many of the creative problem solving strategies do you already use?
2. How did you do on the Nine-Dot Exercise on page 37? If you did it correctly, why did you succeed? If you had trouble, why do you think that it was hard for you?
3. Try these other perception exercises and discuss your results:

a. What do you see in this picture?   **b.** What symbol is in the middle?

A
121314
C

Expressions

Collocations for Discussing Creative Problem Solving

Collocations are words that are frequently used together. Here are some collocations from the two readings in the chapter. They relate to creative problem-solving behavior.

(be) in a creative state of mind   **open your mind to**
extend the boundaries of   **suspend judgment**
generate ideas   **tolerate ambiguity**
judging the merit of   **unlock your mind**

Examples:
The purpose of brainstorming is to **generate ideas** without judging them.
Critical thinkers tend to **suspend judgment** when they encounter new ideas.

Practice

A. Find and underline the collocations in the box above in "Preparing Your Mind for Problem Solving" and "Creative Problem Solving."

B. Now use some of them to complete the sentences. Some collocations from the box work in more than one sentence, and you do not need to use all of them. Pay attention to the words surrounding the collocation to make sure that each sentence is grammatical.

1. If you can _____, then you are comfortable when things aren't completely clear.

2. When you _____, you force yourself not to have an opinion until you get all the information.

3. Brainstorming is generating ideas without _____ the ideas.

4. Another way to say "_____" is "free your mind."

5. A positive way to start the problem-solving process is to _____.

6. It's best to solve problems when you are _____.

Internet Research

Evaluating URLs in Search Results

When you do an Internet search, look carefully at the URL—the website address for the result. URLs include an abbreviation that tells you the organization responsible for the website. These include:

.com   .edu   .gov   .org

The abbreviation **.com** is usually for a store or a business; **.edu** is for an educational institution, such as a college or university; **.gov** is for a government agency; and **.org** is for a nonprofit organization such as a charity.

Check the URL to decide if the result has the information that you want. The abbreviation may be at the end or in the middle of the URL. For example, if you use the keywords "problem solving skills," you might find these URLs in your results:

> www.falcon.jmu.**edu**/~ramseyil/critical.htm
> www.qualitytrainingportal.**com**

Which website should you look at first? Look for the one that has an **.edu** in it. It's probably a school and is more likely to have free information for students. The one that has a **.com** in it may be selling something.

Practice

Practice evaluating URLs. Follow these steps:

1. Do a search for "problem solving" or "problem solving skills."
2. Look at the URLs on the first page of your results and pick one or two that you think will have good information.
3. Go to the websites and check them. Were you right? Check some that you think come from a business. Were you right?
4. Print your search results page. Circle the useful URLs and underline the ones that weren't useful. Bring the page to class and discuss your experience.

Write About It

Write about creative problem solving. Choose one of these topics:

► Describe the most difficult problem to solve, in your opinion. Explain why it is so difficult.
► Describe a problem that you had to solve recently and explain how you solved it.

Use five words and expressions from this chapter. Also, try to use your Internet research.

On Your Own

Project

Solve a problem.

Step 1: Prepare

Describe a problem on an index card or small piece of paper. It can be a personal problem (for example, with school, work, romance, or health) that you've had or a world problem (for example, hunger or poverty); or any other challenging problem. Collect the problems and put them in a hat or a box. Get into small groups. Choose someone in your group to pick a problem out of the hat. Read the problem out loud to your group.

Step 2: Solve a Problem

In your groups, decide how to solve the problem. Use the creative problem solving strategies you read about on pages 36–38. For example, the person with the problem could brainstorm, change his or her routine, or treat the problem as a game. Take notes in the box below on how you solved the problem (for example, the strategies you used) and your solution to the problem. Evaluate your process: was it effective? Why or why not?

Problem: _____

Problem Solving Strategies Used: _____

_____

_____

_____

Solution: _____

_____

Evaluation: _____

_____

_____

Step 3: Follow-Up

Present your problem and solution to the class. Discuss the strategies you used. Evaluate each other's solution. Can you think of additional solutions?

Wrap Up

How Much Do You Remember?

Check your new knowledge. In this chapter you learned facts, words, and expressions. You also learned reading skills and you practiced writing. Complete the following to check what you remember.

1. Give three characteristics of critical thinkers. _____

   _____

2. What are three strategies for creative problem solving? _____

   _____

3. Why is it a good idea to look at the title and headings of a textbook chapter before you read it?

   _____

   _____

4. What are two ways to take notes on something that you've read? _____

   _____

5. Use *is fundamental to* in a sentence. _____

   _____

6. Use *tolerate ambiguity* in a sentence. _____

   _____

7. What do you look for in a URL if you want information from an educational institution?

   _____

Second Timed Readings

Now reread "Preparing Your Mind for Problem Solving" and "Creative Problem Solving." Time each reading separately. Write your times in the Timed Reading Chart on page 232.

Crossword Puzzle

Complete the crossword puzzle to practice some words and expressions from this chapter.

CLUES

Across →
1. Relevant
5. Evaluate
8. Having many parts
10. Unwilling
11. Over a long period of time

Down ↓
2. You can do this if you feel comfortable even when you don't have all the facts.
3. Have an open mind
4. Curious
5. Give up on; forget about
6. People usually are not aware of their _____ mind.
7. Trapped by
9. A discovery

UNIT 2 Business

What is Business?

Business includes accounting, finance, management, marketing, and technology. Communication and ethical behavior are important aspects of business. Other areas of business include:

- brand management
- business analysis
- corporate finance
- electronic commerce systems
- small business management
- information systems
- international business

The earliest business people were traders in the ancient world. Some highlights in the history of business include the invention of paper money around 900 A.D.; the Industrial Revolution of the 19th century; and the first Masters in Business Administration (MBA) program, which began at New York University in 1900.

SOME FAMOUS BUSINESS PEOPLE

Akio Morita—Japanese founder of Sony, 1921–1999

Ingvar Kamprad—Swedish founder of Ikea, 1926–

Carlos Slim Helu—Mexican owner of Telmex, 1940–

Oprah Winfrey—American entertainment executive, 1954–

Bill Gates—American founder of Microsoft, 1955–

Margaret "Meg" Whitman—American president and CEO of eBay, 1957–

Business and You

The study of business is helpful not only in business, but also in art, engineering, medicine, biotechnology, travel, and hospitality.

Do you want to study business? Ask yourself these questions:

- Do I like to make decisions and take action?
- Do I like to analyze situations?
- Am I interested in an international career?
- Do I communicate well with people?
- Can I handle stress well?

CHAPTER PREVIEW

In this chapter, you'll:

Content
▶ learn what Bill Gates says about email
▶ learn how to make an oral presentation

Reading Skills
▶ prepare for reading by connecting with the topic
▶ paraphrase the ideas of others

Vocabulary Skills
▶ use words and expressions for talking about written and oral communication
▶ use collocations for business communication

Writing Skills
▶ write and respond to emails
▶ write about how you feel about giving oral presentations

Internet Skills
▶ learn how to scan a webpage

There is no single thing more important in our efforts to achieve meaningful work and fulfilling relationships than to learn to practice the art of communication. 🐌

— *Max DePree (CEO, author of books on leadership, b. 1924)*

SHORT SURVEY

In communicating with others, I feel the most comfortable when I'm:

❏ face-to-face

❏ using the phone

❏ writing a letter

❏ writing an email

❏ making an oral presentation to a group

❏ other: _____

Reading 1:
What does Bill Gates say about email? Read "Email" and find out.

Reading 2:
What are some tips for making a good oral presentation? Find out in "Making an Oral Presentation."

What do you think?

Answer the questions in the box below. Then ask a partner the questions. Write your partner's answers in the box. Compare your answers.

Email and You		
	My Answers	**My Partner's Answers**
Do you check your email every day? If yes, how many times a day?		
On average, how many emails do you send a day?		
About how much time do you spend on email every day?		
Are most of your emails a response to ones you've received, or do you start the correspondence?		
What percentage of your emails are for work or school communication?		
What percentage of your emails are for personal communication?		
What do you usually use email for (e.g., to make plans or gossip)?		
What do you like about email?		
What do you not like about email?		

Reading 1: Email

Before You Read

Preview

A. The title of Reading 1 is "Email." What do you think you will learn in this reading? Discuss your ideas with a partner.

B. Here are some situations where people need to communicate. Read the situations and decide which is the best means of communication for each situation. Check the appropriate box. Compare and discuss your answers with a partner.

Situations	Face-to-Face	Email	Phone	Letter
Finding out about a homework assignment you missed				
Asking your teacher why you got a certain grade				
Planning a meeting with a friend				
Asking a friend for a ride to school				
Making or canceling a doctor's appointment				
Telling someone that you are in love with him or her				
Telling a boy- or girlfriend that you want to end the relationship				
Telling someone that you are angry with him or her				
Applying for a job				
Making plans to go to a movie				
Planning a meeting at work/school				
Making an agenda for a meeting at work/school				

Vocabulary

Here are some words from "Email." Match each word in the oval with the correct definition. Write the letter of the correct answer on the line.

a. concise   d. distribute   g. niceties   j. vehicle
b. conventions e. efficient   h. persuasive
c. distinctive f. interaction   i. urgency

_____ **1.** in an effective way; without waste, expense, or unnecessary effort

_____ **2.** give out, pass out, deliver

_____ **3.** powerful; able to make people change their minds

_____ **4.** short, brief

_____ **5.** pleasant or polite behaviors

_____ **6.** a way to transmit ideas

_____ **7.** exchange of information or ideas

_____ **8.** accepted ways of doing something

_____ **9.** unique

_____ **10.** importance; a need for prompt action

> The newest computer can merely compound, at speed, the oldest problem in the relations between human beings, and in the end the communicator will be confronted with the old problem, of what to say and how to say it. ❧
>
> — *Edward R. Murrow (American journalist, 1908–1965)*

As you read, think about this question:
▶ What are the advantages and disadvantages of email according to Bill Gates?

🎧 Email

Email is one of the most popular means of communication. Students email their friends, their parents, and their professors. Some people start (and end) romances via email. Others find jobs and do their work via email.

5　At work, people see email as simply a quick way to distribute a memo or send a letter. Email has its own conventions, opportunities, and risks.

John Seabrook, writing an article for *The New Yorker* (January 10, 1994) on Microsoft, realized he could email the 10　company's chairman and guru, Bill Gates. He sent the following message:

Bill Gates

> Dear Bill,
>
> I am the guy who's writing an article about you for *The New Yorker*. It occurs to me that we ought to be able to do some of the work through E-mail. Which raises this fascinating question—what kinds of understanding of another person can E-mail give you?....
>
> 15　You could begin by telling me what you think is unique about E-mail as a form of communication.

Within 18 minutes, Seabrook received the following response from Gates.

> Email is a unique communication vehicle for a lot of reasons. However E-mail is not a substitute for direct interaction....
>
> 20　There are people who I have corresponded with for months before actually meeting them—people at work and otherwise. If someone isn't saying something of interest it's easier to not respond to their mail than it is not to answer the phone. In fact I give out my home phone number to almost no one but my E-mail address is known very broadly. I am the only person who reads my E-mail so no one has to worry about embarrassing themselves or going

25 **around people when they send a message. Our email [at Microsoft Corporation] is completely secure...**

E-mail helps out with other types of communication. It allows you to exchange a lot of information in advance of a meeting and make the meeting far more valuable...

30 **Email is not a good way to get mad at someone since you can't interact. You can send friendly messages very easily since they are harder to misinterpret.**

Since Bill Gates may be the world's most famous and successful user of email, it's worth noting how this response differs from normal written communication. The style falls halfway between writing and conversation: the dots suggest con-
35 versational pauses rather than completed thoughts, *E-mail* becomes *Email*, punctuation is minimal, and there's no formal salutation or conclusion. As Seabrook deduces, "Social niceties are not what Bill Gates is about . . . Good spelling is not what Bill Gates is about either."

More interestingly, Gates' interaction with Seabrook suggests what makes
40 email communication distinctive. It can be used as a non-personal communication that allows the recipient to judge timing and urgency according to her own situation and needs. Email conventions allow brief, efficient exchanges of information or instruction that don't require the time used up by social niceties. Exchanges can be briefer and more idiomatic. They depend less on paragraph
45 building and persuasive argument than on concise information and sharing. Two people in different parts of a building or different parts of the world can almost instantly alert each other to new facts, situations, or job instructions.

Word Count: 556

Source: *Management Communication: Principals and Practices* (Hattersley and McJannet)

Timed Reading

Read "Email" again. Read at a comfortable speed. Time your reading. Write your time in the Timed Reading Chart on page 233.

Start time: _____

End time: _____

My reading time: _____

After You Read

Comprehension

1. What is the main idea of the passage "Email"? _____

   _____

2. Who is John Seabrook? What did he do? _____

   _____

   _____

3. What was Seabrook's question to Bill Gates? _____

   _____

   _____

4. Compare how Bill Gates feels about email and the phone. _____

   _____

   _____

5. What does Bill Gates feel you can judge with email that you can't decide as easily with the

   phone? _____

   _____

6. How do emails compare with other messages, according to the passage? _____

   _____

   _____

Talk About It

Discuss a time when using email worked
very well for you and a time when it
didn't.

Reading 2: Making an Oral Presentation

Before You Read

Reading Skills

Connecting with the Topic

Connecting with the topic of a reading is a good way to get ready to read it. It helps you to stay focused while you read and to understand more of what you're reading. Connecting with the topic means thinking about what you already know about it, deciding what you want to learn about it, and predicting what it will be about. Follow these steps to connect with the topic:

1. Ask yourself questions about the topic. What do you already know about it? What don't you know?

2. Connect your own interests and needs with the reading. Is it related to anything you've read about, done, seen, or studied? Why might you need to know about this topic?

3. Make predictions about the reading even before you begin reading. What information might it include?

Here's an example:

Topic: Business Communication

Questions: What do I know about business? What do I know about communication? What do I know about business communication?

My Interests and Needs: I want to succeed on the job. At work, I will need to communicate well with people. I want to learn to communicate well.

Prediction: This chapter might tell me how to communicate in the business world. It may talk about oral and written communication. It may describe successful business communication and/or unsuccessful business communication. It may tell me stories about famous people who have been successful and how they communicate, what they like and don't like. There may be a contrast between business communication and personal communication.

Practice

Reading 2 is about making an oral presentation. Work with a partner. Practice connecting with this topic. Ask questions, think about your interests and needs, and make predictions about the reading. Record your thoughts in the following chart.

Topic: Making an oral presentation	
My Questions	My Partner's Questions
My Interests and Needs	My Partner's Interests and Needs
My Predictions	My Partner's Predictions

Preview

A. The title of Reading 2 is "Making an Oral Presentation." Use your notes from the chart above to predict at least four ideas about making an oral presentation that you and your partner think the reading will cover.

_____

_____

_____

_____

B. Complete each sentence below with the correct word.

| allotted | convey | manage | self-confident |
| attractive | eliminate | pace | well-groomed |

1. Robert makes brightly colored, easy-to-read PowerPoint slides for his presentations. His

   _____ slides always grab the audience's attention.

2. Chris likes meeting new people. He's outgoing and sure of himself. People like his

   _____ manner.

3. When you are giving an oral presentation, you must look and act like a professional in your

   field. If you _____ a professional image, people will listen to you and

   respect you.

4. Jane had only 30 minutes for her presentation, so she couldn't discuss everything she wanted

   to. To stay within her _____ time, she shortened her presentation.

5. When Jane shortened her presentation, she had to _____ some of her

   ideas.

6. John always wears a clean, pressed suit and has a neat haircut because his boss feels that

   being _____ is important.

7. It's difficult to understand someone who speaks quickly. Therefore, it's important to speak at

   a slow _____ in a presentation.

8. Some people get very nervous when they speak in public. Once they can

   _____ their nervousness, their presentation style improves.

As you read, think about this question:
▶ What can you do to prepare for and make a good oral presentation?

Making an Oral Presentation

Most employers agree that oral communication is a very important job skill. Workers, from assemblers to managers and CEOs, need to be able to make oral presentations. There are many
5 tips to help you prepare for and deliver a presentation. Let's look at some of them.

Preparing for a Presentation

In preparing for a presentation, you should analyze your audience, develop your presenta-
10 tion, prepare notes, and convey a professional image.

Analyzing the Audience. The first step is to analyze the audience. You should learn everything you can about your audience, including their knowledge of and interest in the subject. This will help you plan what to say. Here are some tips to help you analyze your audience:

15 1. Determine the occasion for your presentation. Is it a staff meeting? A birthday party? A retirement banquet?
   2. Respect your audience. This means remain within the allotted time.
   3. Put yourself in the shoes of the people who will be listening to your presentation and ask, "Would this speech be interesting to me?"
20 4. Find out the gender, job titles, education, interests, and general age range of the audience.
   5. Find out how many people will attend so that you can prepare enough handouts.

Developing Your Presentation. The second step in preparing a presentation is
25 developing the content of your speech. Whatever your topic, you should always have a strong introduction and conclusion. A brief, but strong, introduction grabs your audience's attention and gives a clear understanding of what you intend to talk about. Most audiences will remember about five major points. Have a con-

clusion that ends on a positive note. A strong conclusion summarizes your major
points and helps the audience remember what you said. The percentage of time
for each section of a good presentation breaks down as follows:

Introduction	15%
Body	70%
Conclusion	15%

Here are some tips to help you develop your presentation:

- Brainstorm ideas.
- Outline the content.
- Keep the organization simple.
- Do research. A good guideline is to know ten times more about your subject than you are able to discuss during the allotted time. This extra knowledge will help you answer questions and feel self-confident.
- Use repetition to emphasize main points.
- Summarize after each main point.
- Use illustrations and examples to help your audience relate to your content.
- Use humor only if you are comfortable with it. When trying to decide whether or not to tell a particular joke, use the following general rule: when in doubt, leave it out.

Preparing Notes. After you have analyzed your audience and developed the presentation, you should prepare your notes. Here are some tips on preparing to give your presentation:

- Develop speaking notes—words or phrases to remind you of the main points of your presentation.
- If possible, use presentation software such as PowerPoint for your speaking notes or outline. This gives you freedom of movement and keeps the audience focused.
- Print your notes on numbered index cards.
- Practice at least three times in front of a mirror, friend, or family member.

Conveying a Professional Image. You want to look professional when you give your presentation. The following tips should help you convey a professional image:

- Be real, be sincere, and be yourself.
- Be well-groomed. Make sure that your hair and clothes are neat.
- Decide what you will wear for your presentation in time to have your clothes cleaned and pressed.

Delivering Your Presentation

Now, you are ready to actually deliver your presentation. You should greet your audience and speak to them in a friendly tone. The audience has three expectations: that you do not read your presentation, that your speech will be useful and/or interesting, and that you will end on time. Here are some hints on how to deliver your presentation:
- Don't read it. Reading or memorizing it makes you seem unprepared or insincere.
- Be energetic, enthusiastic, and sincere.
- Maintain eye contact.
- Speak at a slow pace and pause occasionally. Silence can be an effective way to get your audience's attention.
- Repeat important points. The audience is more likely to remember details they hear more than once.

Overcoming Nervousness. If you have stage fright, remember that nervousness is normal and that you are not alone in this emotion. Most people list the fear of speaking in public as their number one fear. Experienced speakers do not eliminate stage fright, but they learn how to live with it and how to manage it. Following are some suggestions for managing anxiety:
- Prepare adequately: The key to conquering stage fright is preparation.
- Master your content and visual aids to raise your self-confidence.

- Because much of the anxiety comes as you begin your presentation, make sure that you are especially prepared with a very strong opening.
- Know the audience. Go to the room early, and talk with the members of your audience. Introduce yourself to those whom you do not know, and have an informal conversation with those you already know.
- While in the rest room or other private place, loosen up by bending from the waist and letting your hands and arms hang limp.
- Just before you get up to speak, slowly take three deep breaths to help you relax.
- When you are speaking, focus on your topic and audience.

100

105

Giving oral presentations is an important skill. Give as many oral presentations as you can. Each speaking experience will help you improve your presentation skills.

Word Count: 557

Source: *Communicating in the Workplace* (Dombeck, Camp, and Satterwhite.)

Timed Reading

Read "Making an Oral Presentation" again. Read at a comfortable speed. Time your reading. Write your time in the Timed Reading Chart on page 233.

Start time: _____

End time: _____

My reading time: _____

Main Idea

What four things should you do to give a good oral presentation?

_____

_____

_____

_____

Reading Skills

Paraphrasing

Paraphrasing is putting other people's ideas into your own words. It's a useful reading skill because if you can paraphrase an author's ideas, it means that you really understand them. When you paraphrase an author's ideas either orally or in writing, it can also help you retain important information.

Strategies for paraphrasing include using synonyms for the original words and using a different sentence structure than the original. Here's an example from "Email" on pages 54–55:

Original: Within 18 minutes, Seabrook received the following response from Gates: "Email is a unique communication vehicle for a lot of reasons. However E-mail is not a substitute for direct interaction."

Paraphrase: Soon, Seabrook got an answer from Bill Gates. Gates said that email is a distinctive means of communication for many reasons, although it does not replace a face-to-face conversation.

Notice that the paraphrase combines some of the sentences in the original. It also uses synonyms (for example, *received the following response* becomes *got an answer*) and reported speech (*Gates said that . . .*) instead of a quote.

Practice

Practice paraphrasing some of the ideas in "Making an Oral Presentation." Read the original words and write a paraphrase on the lines. Use synonyms, vary the sentence structure, and combine sentences, if possible.

1. Most employers agree that oral communication is a very important job skill. In other words, if you want to do well on the job, you need to be successful at communicating with others.

   _____

   _____

2. If you have stage fright, remember that nervousness is normal and that you are not alone in this emotion. Most people list the fear of speaking in public as their number one fear.

   _____

   _____

3. Because much of the anxiety comes as you begin your presentation, make sure that you are especially prepared with a very strong opening.

   _____

   _____

Getting the Details

Answer the following questions on a separate piece of paper.

1. According to the author, why should you analyze the audience when you are preparing a presentation?

2. According to the author, why should you always have a strong introduction and conclusion to your presentation?

3. What's the "rule" about using humor in a presentation?

4. Why should you use a software program such as PowerPoint when giving a presentation?

5. How do experienced speakers deal with nervousness?

Vocabulary

A. Here are some more words from "Making an Oral Presentation." Find them in the reading and circle them.

Nouns	Verbs	Adjective
assemblers	loosen	backup
CEO	master	
gender		
retirement		

B. Now use them to complete the sentences.

1. Ashley wants to _____ the topic of his presentation, so she's learning as much as he can about it.

2. Before he learned English well, Tran put computer parts together. All the

   _____ he worked with were non-native speakers of English.

3. "The person's _____ doesn't matter to me. I will hire the best person for the job, male or female," said Ms. Brown.

   _____ doesn't matter to me."

4. Cathy became the Chief Executive Officer of her company at the age of 34. Everyone was

   impressed to see such a young _____.

5. Jeff said, "Janet, will you give a speech at my _____ party. I stop working next week."

6. The second copy of Ken's presentation is his _____ in case he spills coffee on the original.

7. To _____ the muscles of his neck, Ken bends his head to the left and right before he begins a speech.

Talk About It

Discuss this question. Which of the ten points on how to deliver a presentation do you think are most important? Why?

Expressions

Collocations for Talking about Communication

Collocations are words that are frequently used together. When you learn collocations, notice how they are used in a sentence. Notice also the entire expression. For example, notice which verbs and prepositions are in it.

Here are some collocations from the two readings in this chapter that relate to communication.

absorb information	fear of speaking
brainstorm ideas	have stage fright
deliver your presentation	keep the audience focused
ends on a positive note	via email

Examples:

Psychologists say that being interested in a topic makes it easier **to absorb the information** about that topic.

Audiences love Harry Schaffner's speeches because he always **ends on a positive note**.

Practice

A. Find and underline the collocations from the box in "Email" and "Making an Oral Presentation."

B. Now use some of them to complete the sentences.

1. Rich used to _____ and didn't want to get up in front of groups, but he overcame it by taking every opportunity to speak in front of people.

2. If you _____ with friends to prepare for your presentation, then you will come up with more ideas.

3. Sandy doesn't like to talk on the phone. He would rather communicate

   _____.

4. The number one fear for most Americans is the _____ in public.

5. Stand up straight, smile at the audience when you _____, and your audience will be interested.

6. To _____, prepare attractive slides. That way, you will maintain their attention during your presentation.

How to Read a Homepage

Reading webpages uses scanning skills. Scanning is moving your eyes quickly over a page to find specific information. Scanning the homepage—the main page of a website—can help you decide quickly if the site is useful to you. Scanning also helps you find out where to go to get the information that you need. To do this, you scan for the following:

▶ **Page Title:** When you get to a homepage, scan for the page title first. It should describe the information on that particular page. It may be in a large font, at the top middle or top left of the page. The page may also have subheadings. These will tell you the main ideas of any sections on the page.

▶ **Navigation Links:** Next scan for "navigation links," links to other pages. These tell you the main areas or sections of the site. Navigation links are usually on the left-hand side of the page, at the top, or across the bottom. Navigation links should match the titles of the pages that they link to.

Practice

Look for a website on public speaking or any topic that interests you and go to the homepage. Scan the page to answer the questions below. Bring a copy of the page to class and discuss it with a partner.

1. Is there a page title? What is it? Where are the navigation links? List some.
2. In your opinion, is it easy to locate information on this page? Why or why not?

Write About It

Write about business communication. Choose one of these topics:

▶ Write an email to a classmate. Describe how you feel about giving an oral presentation. Write a response to the email that you receive.
▶ Write a paragraph in which you explain your techniques for overcoming nervousness.

Use five words and expressions from this chapter. Also, try to use your Internet research.

On Your Own

Project

Give a five-minute oral presentation on a topic of your choice.

Step 1: Prepare

Decide on a topic. Choose something you know well. Here are some ideas:

▶ Demonstrate something you know how to do.

▶ Tell the class about your country or about a particular custom in your country.

▶ Give advice (e.g., on how to stay healthy, how to save money, etc).

Be sure to limit the topic so that it will fit within the time limit. For example, you may wish to demonstrate how to change a guitar string, rather than how to play the guitar. Brainstorm ideas, do research, and outline your content. Follow the suggestions in "Making an Oral Presentation." Practice your speeches in groups.

Step 2: Give the Presentation

Give your presentation in small groups. Have your group members evaluate it. Use the evaluation form below.

Speaker: _____ Evaluator: _____	Good	OK	Needs Improvement	Comments
1. Speaker did not read speech and maintained eye contact.				
2. Speaker was energetic.				
3. Speaker repeated important points.				
4. Speaker had good visual aids.				
5. Speaker could answer questions from the audience.				

Step 3: Follow-Up

Discuss your presentations. Which were interesting? What made them interesting? What will you do differently the next time that you give a presentation?

Wrap Up

How Much Do You Remember?

Check your new knowledge. In this chapter you learned facts, words, and expressions. You also learned reading skills and you practiced writing. Complete the following to check what you remember.

1. If someone says your email is *concise*, what do they mean? _____

    _____

2. Why does Bill Gates like email? _____

    _____

3. How do you make attractive PowerPoint slides for an oral presentation? _____

    _____

4. What percentage of time should you use for the introduction, the body, and the conclusion of

    your presentation? _____

    _____

5. How can you *convey* a professional image? _____

    _____

6. Paraphrase the following: "The poor speak very fast with quick movements to attract attention. The rich move slowly and they speak slowly; they don't need to get your attention because they've already got it." Michael Caine (British actor, b. 1933)

    _____

    _____

    _____

7. What is one way to scan the homepage of a website? _____

    _____

Second Timed Readings

Now reread "Email" and "Making an Oral Presentation." Time each reading separately. Write your times in the Timed Reading Chart on page 233.

Crossword Puzzle

Complete the crossword puzzle to practice some words and expressions from this chapter.

CLUES

Across →
1. Convincing
5. Have control over
9. Express
11. Jane's nervous about giving a presentation. She has _____

Down ↓
2. Period when you stop working
3. Feeling sure about yourself
4. According to Gates, email is a unique communication _____
6. Short; brief

7. Give out
8. Great importance
10. Using electronic mail
12. Male or female

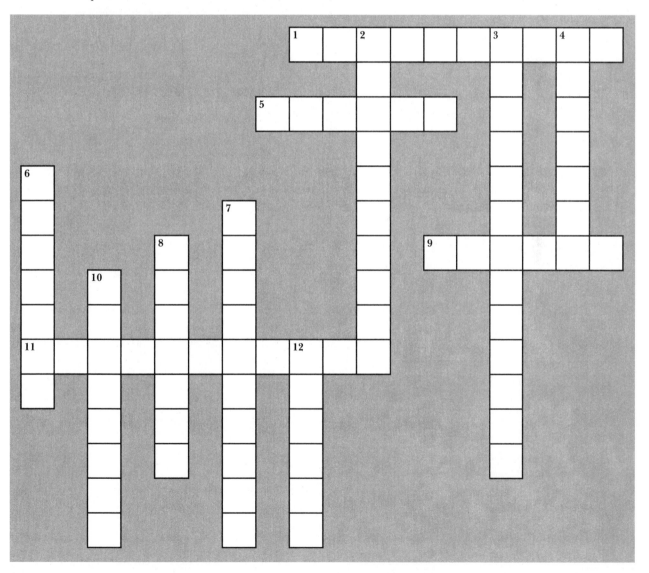

CHAPTER 4

Business Ethics

CHAPTER PREVIEW

In this chapter, you'll:

Content
▶ read an introduction to ethics
▶ find out about a company that is dedicated to following ethical principles

Reading Skills
▶ preview by reading the introduction and conclusion to a reading
▶ make inferences

Vocabulary Skills
▶ use words and expressions for discussing ethics, business, and business ethics
▶ use collocations for discussing business ethics

Writing Skills
▶ describe an ethical issue you had to deal with and how you dealt with it
▶ describe your personal code of ethics

Internet Skills
▶ locate on the Internet and read companies' codes of ethics

> To know what is right and not to do it is the worst cowardice. 🐚
>
> — *Confucius (Chinese teacher, philosopher, and political theorist, 551–479 B.C.)*

SHORT SURVEY

I learned the difference between right and wrong from:

❑ my family

❑ my friends

❑ my religion

❑ reading books

❑ other: _____

Reading 1:

What are *ethics*? How do businesses make ethical decisions? "Ethics: An Introduction" has the answers.

Reading 2:

What ethical challenges has one major corporation faced and how has it dealt with them? Read "Ethics in Business: Hewlett-Packard" to find out.

What do you think?

How much do you already know about business ethics? Read each statement in the box below and circle *Agree* if you agree or *Disagree* if you disagree. Then discuss your answers with a partner.

Business Ethics: What I Already Know

1.	Business ethics are different from general ethics.	Agree	Disagree
2.	Ethics are relative—different for different situations or people.	Agree	Disagree
3.	Companies face ethical questions on a daily basis.	Agree	Disagree
4.	Thinking about ethics is something that a company does at the beginning when it's starting up. After things have been decided, it doesn't need to think about ethical issues again.	Agree	Disagree
5.	A company should behave ethically with its employees but not necessarily with the community in which it is located.	Agree	Disagree
6.	A company's code of ethics should have policies on:		
	equal opportunity	Agree	Disagree
	sexual harassment	Agree	Disagree
	the environment	Agree	Disagree
	providing information about customers	Agree	Disagree
	political affiliation	Agree	Disagree
	health and safety	Agree	Disagree
	gift giving	Agree	Disagree
7.	A good test for making an ethical decision in the workplace is how you feel about it afterwards. If you feel good, you made the right decision. If you feel bad, you probably didn't.	Agree	Disagree

Reading 1: Ethics: An Introduction

Before You Read

Preview

A. The title of Reading 1 is "Ethics: An Introduction." What kind of information might an introduction to ethics include? Discuss your ideas with a partner.

> Relativity applies to physics, not ethics. 🐌
>
> — *Albert Einstein (German-born American theoretical physicist, 1879–1955)*

B. Answer the following questions. They are based on some important ethical issues. Compare and discuss your answers with a partner.

  1. Should animals be used in scientific experiments?

  2. Should humans be cloned?

  3. Should a person's DNA (genetic information) be private?

  4. Is it O.K. for athletes to take drugs to enhance (improve) their performance?

  5. Does a company have the right to read its employees' emails?

  6. Is Internet file-sharing (that is, downloading to your computer other people's copies of music, movies, or software) O.K.?

  7. Is it O.K. to photocopy textbook chapters to give to a friend?

  8. Is it O.K. to have a friend take a standardized test (for example, the TOEFL or the SAT) for you?

  9. Is it O.K. for a company to manufacture its product in a country that has fewer environmental protection laws than those of the country in which it sells its product?

  10. Is it O.K. to shop at a store that sells products made in countries that have bad human rights records?

Discuss:
▶ How did you arrive at your decisions? That is, why did you answer as you did? On what did you base your answer?
▶ How do you account for any differences between your answers and your partner's?

Vocabulary

Here are some words and expressions from "Ethics: An Introduction." Match them with the highlighted words or expressions in the sentences. Write the letter of the correct answer on the line.

a. absolute   c. consistent with   e. impact   g. perspective
b. confront   d. financial sums   f. intentional   h. shifted

_____ 1. Some companies lose huge **amounts of money** in lawsuits because of the unethical behavior of their employees.

_____ 2. Sue is a very ethical person. Her ethical beliefs are **not in conflict with** her religion.

_____ 3. For example, Sue's **view** on helping the poor comes directly from the teachings of her religion.

_____ 4. Paul noticed that his co-worker did something unethical. After work, he plans to **meet with and tell** his co-worker that her behavior was wrong.

_____ 5. Some people think that ethical beliefs should be **unchanging**; others feel that ethics are relative.

_____ 6. When Chris copied a research paper he found on the Internet, it was **deliberate**. He planned to do it, even though he knew it was wrong.

_____ 7. During ancient times, the emphasis on morality **changed** from inner character to overt behavior.

_____ 8. Ethical decisions have an **effect** on all aspects of a person's life, from their private life to their work life.

> The time is always right to do right. ≉
>
> — *Martin Luther King, Jr.*
> *(African-American civil rights leader and Nobel laureate, 1929–1968)*

As you read, think about this question:
► What is one way of making ethical decisions?

Aristotle

🎧 Ethics: An Introduction

Imagine that you are a salesperson for a large company. You learn that the equipment you sell is faulty (it doesn't work properly) and could be dangerous. You have a spouse who needs medical treatment. This treatment is expensive, so your job, which gives you medical insurance, is very important to you. You 5 believe that if you confront your employer about the faulty equipment, you will lose your job. What would you do?

This is an example of an ethical decision. Ethics is the branch of philosophy concerned with moral behavior. It is the study of moral judgments. Moral judgments are judgments about what is right and wrong.

10 ## The Origins of Ethics

The word "ethics" is derived from the Greek word *ethos*. Originally, *ethos* meant "a dwelling place." For the Greek philosopher Aristotle, *ethos* meant "an *inner* dwelling place," or what is now called "inner character." The Latin translation of *ethos* is *mos, moris,* from which we get the English word "moral." In Roman 15 times, the emphasis on morality shifted from internal character to overt behavior—acts, habits, and customs. In more recent times, ethics has been viewed as an overall human concern. Some of the main issues that ethicists consider are the basis of moral values and whether morals are absolute or relative.

Ethical Questions

20 Ethical questions are important in both work life and personal life. Ethics is a difficult subject because it forces people to think about moral questions with difficult answers. This is true now more than ever before. Consider the type of ethical questions that people are faced with today. How would you answer these questions?

- *The intentional creation of new forms of life*. Animals have already been cloned.
25 But is this right? Should people be cloned? If so, who should be cloned?
- *Space exploration*. Should people be exploring space? Is it right to spend huge financial sums on space exploration?
- *Nuclear energy*. What should be done about atomic energy? Can we ever justify building bombs that can destroy life? Should we only apply our
30 knowledge of nuclear energy to human welfare?

Stakeholder Analysis

Our personal ethical decisions about our everyday life affect us and other people around us. In some areas, ethical decisions can affect hundreds, thousands, or even hundreds of thousands of people. One way that people in companies can
35 make ethical decisions is called "stakeholder analysis." "Stakeholders" are all the groups or individuals who are affected by a decision. Stakeholder analysis involves the following nine parts of a decision-making process:

1. **Identification:** What is the ethical issue relevant to the decision?
2. **Facts:** What are the facts?
40 3. **Alternatives:** What are the alternatives? That is, what are the possible solutions to the question or problem?
4. **Stakeholders:** Who has a stake in the outcome? Who will be affected by the decision? What is their relationship to each other and what is their relationship to you?
45 5. **Impact:** What is the impact of each possible alternative on each stakeholder?
6. **Guidance:** Can you discuss the issue with others and get their opinions and perspectives?
7. **Constraints:** Are each of the alternative solutions legal and/or consistent
50 with your organization's policies? Are the alternative solutions moral?
8. **Comfort:** Are you comfortable with the decision?
9. **Assessment:** After you've made the decision, can you assess it and make changes, if necessary?

Word Count: 605

Sources: *The Art of Leadership* (Manning and Curtis) and *Perspectives in Business Ethics* (Hartman)

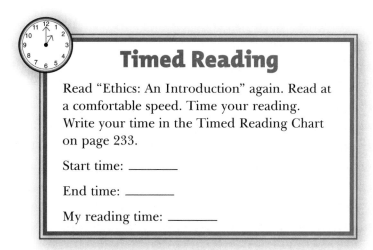

Timed Reading

Read "Ethics: An Introduction" again. Read at a comfortable speed. Time your reading. Write your time in the Timed Reading Chart on page 233.

Start time: _____

End time: _____

My reading time: _____

After You Read

Comprehension

1. Write a statement that expresses the main idea of "Ethics: An Introduction."

   _____

   _____

2. Define *ethics* in your own words.

   _____

   _____

3. How has the meaning of *ethics* changed since it was used in ancient Greece?

   _____

   _____

4. Why does the author give examples of ethical questions in Paragraph 4? Why did the author choose these particular questions?

   _____

   _____

5. Explain in your own words the meaning of *stakeholder*.

   _____

   _____

6. Choose one of the following parts of the stakeholder analysis process and explain what it means in your own words: impact, guidance, or constraints.

   _____

   _____

Reading 2: Ethics in Business: Hewlett-Packard

Before You Read

Preview

A. The title of Reading 2 is "Ethics in Business: Hewlett-Packard." What do you already know about Hewlett-Packard? What kind of business is it? If you are unfamiliar with the company, think about how ethics might be important in a large corporation. Discuss your ideas with a partner.

B. Preview these words and expressions from the reading. Complete each sentence with the correct word or expression.

> adhere to   compliance with   fosters   integrity
> bribes   core values   initiative   through consensus

1. It's important for upper-level managers to _____ their company's ethical guidelines. If they don't follow them, then how can they expect their employees to?

2. _____ the law is one of the most important aspects of ethical behavior for a company. Most people would agree that any behavior that breaks the law is obviously unethical.

3. A good manager _____ creativity in his or her employees. If a manager promotes an atmosphere where creativity is valued, then workers will feel free to think creatively.

4. A company's _____ are the ethical principles that it follows in its day-to-day operations.

5. The marketing group made the decision _____. After much discussion, everyone agreed with the plan.

6. Some cultures do not allow company employees to accept _____. In fact, employees taking money from someone who wants to do business with their company is considered unethical in many parts of the world.

7. Most employers like workers with _____. The ability to do something without being told to do it is a highly desirable characteristic in an employee.

8. Lynn has _____. When she says something, you always know she's telling the truth.

Reading Skills

Using the Introduction and Conclusion to Preview

The introduction and conclusion in a reading often tell you what the reading is about. You can frequently find the main and supporting ideas of a reading in the introduction (usually the first paragraph or paragraphs of a reading). Introductions also often contain general or background information on the topic.

The conclusion often restates the main and supporting ideas of the reading. In fact, a conclusion is often more specific than the introduction, and it usually reviews the most important information in the reading. In addition, a conclusion may point to a new idea related to the topic.

Look at the introduction and conclusion to "Barriers to Critical Thinking" on pages 15–17 of Chapter 1:

Introduction:

Critical thinking helps people solve problems and make good decisions. Uncritical thinking is common. Many people, including smart and well-educated people, find critical thinking difficult. Here is a list of some of the most common barriers to critical thinking: egocentrism (self-centered thinking); face-saving; lack of relevant background information; overpowering emotions; self-deception; self-interested thinking; sociocentrism (group-centered thinking); superstition; and unwarranted assumptions.

Three of these—egocentrism, sociocentrism, and unwarranted assumptions—play an especially powerful role in preventing critical thinking. Let's look at these one at a time.

Conclusion:

There are many barriers to critical thinking. Egocentrism, sociocentrism, and unwarranted assumptions are a few of them. If you know about these barriers, it can help you be a better thinker. This, in turn, can help you at school, at work, and when making decisions in daily life.

Notice how the introduction begins with general information about the topic and ends with a sentence that tells you exactly what to expect in the reading. The main idea is barriers to critical thinking, and the supporting ideas are how three of them (egocentrism, sociocentrism, and unwarranted assumptions) play a role in preventing critical thinking. The conclusion reinforces this by restating the main and supporting ideas. When you combine the information in the introduction with information in the conclusion, you get a clear idea of the main points of a reading before you read it.

Practice

Read the introduction and conclusion to Reading 2 on pages 82–85. The introduction is the first four paragraphs of the reading and the conclusion is the last paragraph of the reading. Then answer the following questions.

1. Find a statement of the main idea at the end of the first paragraph and underline it.

2. Now, paraphrase the main idea in your own words. _____

    _____

3. What other information about the topic is included in the introduction? Is it general information, background information, or both?

    _____

    _____

4. What kind of information is presented in the fourth paragraph? Give examples of the kind of information that may provide support for the main idea.

    _____

    _____

5. Does the conclusion restate the main and supporting ideas of the reading? _____

    What other information does the conclusion contain? _____

    _____

    _____

6. What do you think you will learn about in "Ethics in Business: Hewlett-Packard"?

    _____

    _____

As you read, think about this question:
▶ What are some of Hewlett-Packard's core values?

🎧 Ethics in Business: Hewlett-Packard

Companies are constantly faced with making decisions that can impact large numbers of stakeholders, such as their employees, their
5 customers, the community, and the environment. Most companies develop a code of ethics to guide decision-making and most strive to follow it. Some are more successful
10 than others. One company that is exemplary in its commitment to ethical behavior and its model ethical guidelines is the high-technology company Hewlett-Packard (HP).

HP was founded in 1939 by William Hewlett and David Packard. The direc-
15 tion of the company was set in the 1950s when objectives were developed that provided the foundation for the core values of the organization. Some of HP's early values included:

- providing employment opportunities to employees that include the chance to share in the company's success;
20 - maintaining an organizational environment that fosters individual motivation, initiative, and creativity;
- demonstrating good citizenship by making contributions to the community.

Employees see the values and ethics of the company evidenced in the behavior of the company's managers and executives. The values are part of the com-
25 pany's strong company culture, which is reinforced on a daily basis.

Like many companies, HP is constantly changing and its guiding documents are evolving as well. A recent document entitled "Business Ethics" appears to be a response to the need for clear ethical principles in an era of high-profile corporate scandals. This code of ethics focuses upon integrity and the company's dedication to the principles of honesty, excellence, responsibility, compassion, citizenship, fairness, and respect.

HP is also concerned with social and environmental responsibility. For example, HP requires suppliers to adhere to all laws protecting the environment, worker health and safety, and labor and employment practices in the countries in which they operate. In addition, they must establish management systems that insure compliance with the laws and regulations. It is also developing significant programs to reduce material and energy usage such as recycling programs that focus on "end-of-life" issues—how to deal with its products once they have been discarded.

An HP Digital Village—a neighborhood program that provides free computer training—is one way that HP contributes to the community.

The firm's confidence in and respect for its employees is constantly stressed. Employees are given a great deal of freedom. They select which eight-hour shift they want to work, and can begin at 6, 7, or 8 A.M. HP does not use time clocks. Employees are given specific job objectives and may negotiate with their supervisor to determine how the objectives will be met.

Open communication is stressed. Everyone in the firm is on a first-name basis. Company offices are created using low partitions so that an employee can talk to the person in the next office simply by leaning over the partition. Management strongly encourages open communication both up and down the levels in the firm. HP also has an "Open Door Policy," which gives all employees the right to discuss their concerns with the level of management they feel is appropriate to handle the situation. They can do this without fear of any negative consequences.

HP believes in employees sharing benefits and responsibilities. Equal sharing of rewards through a profit-sharing plan and a stock-purchase plan is stressed. Offices are generally the same size, with supervisors sharing offices with their secretaries. Carpeting is a rarity and parking spaces are generally unassigned. The company fosters a sense of teamwork and partnership in its everyday business operations. Decisions are generally made through consensus and persuasion in small work groups.

65 Honesty and integrity are basic HP core values. HP does not tolerate dishonesty among its employees. Its "Standards of Business Conduct" cites four areas of employee obligations:

1. to HP,
2. to customers,
70 3. to competitors,
4. to suppliers.

Obligations to HP include avoiding conflicts of interest, maintaining the confidentiality of company information, and reporting and avoiding payments (such as bribes) to foreign sales agents or government officials. Customer obligations
75 include fair trade practices and methods of competition, and confidentiality of information. Competitor obligations include maintaining good relations with competitors and obtaining competitor information honestly. Supplier obligations include honoring confidential information. General managers are responsible for their employees' familiarization with the standards.

80 In July 1999, Carly Fiorina was chosen as the first outside president and chief executive of HP. On May 3, 2002, she won a hard-fought battle to merge HP with Compaq Computers to create the second largest computer company. The merger

Carly Fiorina, former CEO of Hewlett-Packard

has resulted in eliminating more than 15,000 people from the combined work-force. Layoffs of that magnitude appear to go against the HP Way. Fiorina left HP in February, 2005. It will be interesting to see what changes new chief executive officers will make and how these changes will impact the firm and the company's dedication to its core values of honesty, excellence, responsibility, compassion, citizenship, fairness, and respect.

85

Word Count: 774

Source: *Business Ethics* (Fritzsche)

Timed Reading

Read "Ethics in Business: Hewlett-Packard" again. Read at a comfortable speed. Time your reading. Write your time in the Timed Reading Chart on page 233.

Start time: _____

End time: _____

My reading time: _____

Main Idea

Write a statement that describes the main and supporting ideas of "Ethics in Business: Hewlett-Packard."

_____

_____

_____

Reading Skills

Making Inferences

When you read, it's important to understand information that the author does not directly state. This is making inferences, or inferring. It's an important critical thinking skill. When you infer something, you make a guess or draw a conclusion based on something that the author *does* state. It's important to remember that an inference is always based on something that is stated in the text.

For example, in "Ethics in Business: Hewlett-Packard," the author states: "Carpeting is a rarity. . ." Why did the author choose this as example of equality? You can infer that the author probably believes that carpeting is a luxury and that a carpeted office is a sign of superiority.

Practice

Make inferences to answer the following questions about "Ethics in Business: Hewlett-Packard."

1. Does the author feel that HP managers behave in an ethical manner? Find and write the information in the text that supports your answer.

_____

_____

_____

2. Does the author think that the merger between HP and Compaq Computers and the resignation of Carly Fiorina might challenge HP ethics? Find and write the information in the text that supports your answer.

_____

_____

_____

Getting the Details

A. Answer the following question.

What does the author think inspired HP to revise its code of ethics and publish a document called "Business Ethics"?

_____

_____

B. Complete the graphic organizer with examples that illustrate ways in which HP lives up to its core values:

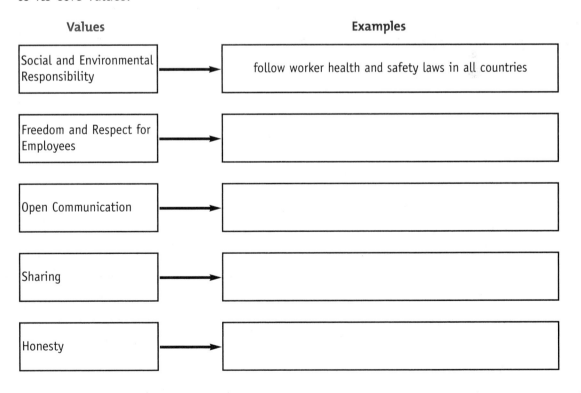

Values	Examples
Social and Environmental Responsibility	follow worker health and safety laws in all countries
Freedom and Respect for Employees	
Open Communication	
Sharing	
Honesty	

Vocabulary

A. Here are some business terms from "Ethics in Business: Hewlett-Packard." Find them in the reading and circle them.

> ### Business Terms
>
> layoffs   partitions   stock-purchase plan
> profit-sharing plan   teamwork

B. Now use them to complete the sentences.

1. When a company has a _____, the employees receive a share of the company's profits.

2. Mary wasn't too happy about all the _____ at her company. The possibility of losing their jobs was making many people nervous.

3. Jack owns a lot of Hewlett-Packard stock because HP has a _____, and Jack worked there for many years.

4. Most companies value _____ over independence, so being able to work cooperatively in a group is a highly desirable skill.

5. Some offices have _____, where half-walls separate workers from each other. Other offices have the open plan, where no walls separate people from each other.

Talk About It

Discuss these questions.

1. What are your personal core values? Give examples of how you behave in accordance with them.
2. If you worked for a large corporation, what kind of core values would you like the company to have? What kind of corporate environment would you like to work in?
3. Have you heard of companies that do or do not follow good core values? Give examples.

Collocations for Discussing Ethics

Collocations are words that are frequently used together. Here are some collocations from the two readings in this chapter. They relate to ethical issues.

avoiding conflicts of interest	**a/the decision-making process**
(the basis of) moral values	**develop a code of ethics**
be concerned with social/	**has/have a stake in the outcome**
environmental responsibility	**honoring confidential information**
the core values	

When you learn collocations, notice how they are used in a sentence. Notice also the entire expression. For example, notice which verbs and prepositions are in it.

Example:

Many companies **develop a code of ethics**, a set of guidelines that they use to make ethical decisions.

Practice

A. Find and underline the collocations in the box above in "Ethics: An Introduction" and "Ethics in Business: Hewlett-Packard."

B. Now use some of them to complete the sentences. You can use some of the expressions more than once.

1. _____ is an important value at many companies. This means that employees don't reveal trade secrets to companies that they do business with.

2. Many companies let employees take part in _____. They let employees give their opinions on decisions.

3. _____ means a corporate employee doesn't get involved in any activity that would either involve disclosing confidential information about or create competition with his or her employer.

4. Religion is the basis of many people's _____.

5. _____ of an organization can tell you a lot about what it would be like to work there.

6. A stakeholder is anyone or any group that _____ of a decision.

Internet Research

Finding Corporate Codes of Ethics on the Internet

Most large corporations publish on their websites information about their values. Core values usually are not on the homepage of the website. However, you can often find them listed on the pages on the website such as *About Us* or *Company Information*. These pages usually contain information about the company's ethics.

For example, if you go to Hewlett-Packard's website (**www.hp.com**), you'll find *Company Information* on the homepage. When you go to that area, you'll see a list of topics. One is *Business Ethics*. This is where HP describes the values that it follows.

Another way to find a company's core values is to do a search using a search engine (such as Google), using keyword combinations such as *hewlett-packard core values* or *"hewlett-packard"* + *"business ethics."*

Note: It is not necessary to capitalize proper nouns in a search engine.

Practice

Practice looking for and reading corporate core values. Try looking for the following:

▶ Find the core values for any large company that interests you. Print them out, and bring them to class. Compare them to HP's core values as described on pages 82–85.
▶ Find and print the core values of two different companies and compare them.
▶ Find Hewlett-Packard's website and compare the information on pages 82–85 with current information about the company. Have the core values changed?

Bring the results of your research to class and discuss them. Discuss how you found the information; for example, which keywords did you use? What links on the homepage took you to the information you were looking for?

Write About It

Write about ethical behavior. Choose one of these topics:

▶ Describe an ethical issue you had to deal with and how you dealt with it.
▶ Describe your personal code of ethics.

Use five words and expressions from this chapter. Also, try to use your Internet research.

On Your Own

Project

Give a presentation on the core values of a corporation. Give examples of how the company practices its core values.

Step 1: Prepare

Choose a company. Find and read information about its core values on its website. Look for examples of how the company practices its values. For example, HP believes in social responsibility, so they have a Digital Village program that gives free computer training to people in the communities in which HP does business. This program is described in the Business Ethics area of their website.

Write notes for your presentation in the box below or on a separate piece of paper. Practice your presentation with a partner. Have your teacher listen to make sure that you are pronouncing words correctly.

Core Values of _____ (company name)

Values: _____

_____

_____

_____

Examples (if any) of how the company practices its values: _____

_____

_____

_____

Step 2: Give the Presentation

Give your presentation in small groups. Take turns speaking. Make eye contact with your audience. The audience should take notes and ask questions afterwards.

Step 3: Follow-Up

Discuss your presentations. Which were interesting? What made them interesting? What will you do differently the next time that you give a presentation?

Wrap Up

How Much Do You Remember?

Check your new knowledge. In this chapter you learned facts, words, and expressions. You also learned reading skills and you practiced writing. Complete the following to check what you remember.

1. What are ethics? What are business ethics? _____

   _____

2. Give a brief definition of *stakeholder analysis.* _____

   _____

3. Give one example of how Hewlett-Packard behaves according to its core values. _____

   _____

4. How do the introduction and conclusion help you to preview a reading? _____

   _____

5. What does it mean to make inferences about something that you have read? _____

   _____

6. What's the difference between *absolute* and *relative ethics?* _____

   _____

7. Use the collocation *have a stake in the outcome* in a sentence. _____

   _____

8. What links on a company's website might lead you to an explanation of their core values? _____

   _____

Second Timed Readings

Now reread "Ethics: An Introduction" and "Business Ethics: Hewlett-Packard." Time each reading separately. Write your times in the Timed Reading Chart on page 233.

Crossword Puzzle

Complete the crossword puzzle to practice some words and expressions from this chapter.

CLUES

Across →

4. Agreement
7. View
10. With purpose; not accidental
11. Unethical gifts or money given to a person or a company

Down ↓

1. Ethical principles
2. The opposite of *relative*
3. Doing something that needs to be done without someone telling you to do it
5. What is your personal _____ of ethics?
6. I have _____ in the outcome of this decision.
7. Walls that separate workers in an office
8. Honoring _____ information means not sharing information with people who shouldn't hear it.
9. When people's jobs are no longer necessary and they are asked to leave a company

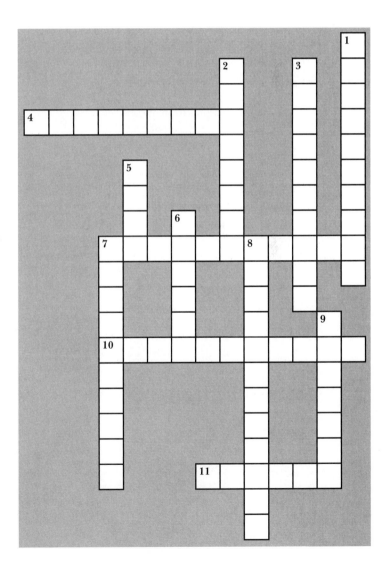

What is Film Studies?

Film studies investigates all aspects of movies. It includes the study of the history of movies, genre films, filmmaking, directors, and screenwriters. Other areas in film studies include:

- Hollywood movies
- documentary movies
- special effects
- film editing
- animation
- film theory and criticism
- women in cinema
- indie (independent) movies
- international films

Many technological advances have contributed to the development of motion pictures, from the invention of photography in the 19th century to the use of digital images in the 21st century.

SOME FAMOUS NAMES IN FILM STUDIES

Eadweard Muybridge—British-born American photographer, 1830–1904

Thomas Edison—American inventor, 1847–1931

Auguste and Louis Lumière—French inventors, 1862–1954 (Auguste); 1864–1948 (Louis)

André Bazin—French film theorist, 1918–1958

Pauline Kael—American film critic, 1919–2001

Lina Wertmuller—Italian director, 1928–

Film Studies and You

The study of film is useful in careers such as filmmaking, teaching, journalism, film archiving, film restoration, and marketing and distribution.

Do you want to study film? Ask yourself these questions:

- Do I like movies?
- Am I interested in the technical aspects of film, such as cinematography?
- Do I like to do research and write?
- Am I interested in the history of film?
- Would I like to work with film archives?
- Do I believe movies should be perserved?

History of Film

CHAPTER PREVIEW

In this chapter, you'll:

Content
▶ read about film history from 1893 to the present
▶ learn about the success of some new Hollywood directors

Reading Skills
▶ use topic sentences to preview a reading
▶ identify facts and opinions

Vocabulary Skills
▶ use words and expressions to discuss directors and filmmaking
▶ use collocations to talk about film history

Writing Skills
▶ describe your personal "film history"

Internet Skills
▶ research film history on the Internet

SHORT SURVEY

I go to the movies:
❏ once a month
❏ three times a month
❏ once a week
❏ twice a week
❏ three or more times a week
❏ other: _____

Reading 1:

What are some important events in the history of movies? Read "Film History Timeline: 1893 to the Present" to find out.

Reading 2:

Have minorities been successful in Hollywood? Find out in "The New Hollywood."

What do you think?

Answer the questions in the box. Then compare your answers with a partner.

My Movie History

1. What is the first movie that you remember seeing? (If you can't remember the first movie you saw, think of one that you remember seeing as a young child.)

   _____

2. How old were you? Who did you see it with? _____

   _____

3. Did you like it? _____

4. Do you remember any details about the movie? If yes, describe the type of movie it was, the plot, and list any actors that you remember.

   _____

   _____

5. Where did you see it? _____

6. If you went to a theater, what kind was it? (Was it large, small, crowded, etc.?) Describe anything else that you remember about the theater.

   _____

   _____

7. Describe anything else that you remember from the experience.

   _____

   _____

Reading 1: Film History Timeline: 1893 to the Present

Before You Read

Preview

A. The title of Reading 1 is "Film History Timeline: 1893 to the Present." What kind of information might it include? What kinds of movies might the timeline include? Discuss your ideas with a partner.

B. How much do you already know about the history of filmmaking? Read the statements. Circle *T* (True) or *F* (False).

1. Photography was invented in the 1800s.   T   F

2. Some of the first movies ever filmed were made in France.   T   F

3. The first American movie studio was located in California.   T   F

4. The first color films appeared in the early 1950s.   T   F

5. The popularity of TV made movie audiences get smaller.   T   F

6. Many women, African Americans, and other minorities had success as filmmakers in the early days of Hollywood filmmaking.   T   F

C. Try to match the movie style with the correct description. Use the highlighted word parts to help you guess.

_____ 1. **Express**ionism   **a.** a movie style that deals with realistic social problems

_____ 2. **Impression**ism   **b.** a very expressive movie style with exaggerated images

_____ 3. Neo**real**ism   **c.** a surreal (unrealistic) movie style with strange or illogical events

_____ 4. **Surreal**ism   **d.** a movie style with impressionist images showing thoughts, perceptions, and impressions

Vocabulary

Here are some words and expressions from "Film History Timeline: 1893 to the Present." Match them with the highlighted words or expressions in the sentences. Write the letter of the correct answer on the line.

a. disrupt   c. inexplicable   e. narrative   g. via flashbacks
b. distorted   d. merge   f. prototype   h. winning recognition

_____ 1. *Star Wars* is a **storytelling** type of movie; it presents the plot in a logical fashion.

_____ 2. Most famous filmmakers in the past were white males. Today, many women, African Americans, and other minorities are **becoming well-known** as filmmakers.

_____ 3. Three major movie companies decided to **combine** to form one new company called Metro-Goldwyn-Mayer, or MGM.

_____ 4. The images in many of the scenes of an expressionist movie are difficult to recognize because they are **unclear**.

_____ 5. *The Great Train Robbery* was the **model** for the classical American film.

_____ 6. Many movie plots explain a character's motives **by showing events that happened in the past**, from before the story began.

_____ 7. Many modern films borrow a technique from surrealism when they **interrupt** the logical flow of events in the story.

_____ 8. For some reason that is **impossible to explain**, a character in an early French surrealist film suddenly disappears.

> Why should people go out and pay money to see bad films when they can stay at home and see bad television for nothing? 🎬
>
> — *Samuel Goldwyn (American director, 1882–1974)*

As You Read

As you read, think about this question:
▶ What are the seven major periods in the history of filmmaking

🎧 Film History Timeline: 1893 to the Present

The history of film begins in the late 1800s. The invention of photography in 1826 led to a series of discoveries that gradually made moving pictures possible. The first films were extremely simple in form and style. They
5 usually consisted of a single shot showing a single action, such as a scenic place or a news event. At the same time, some early filmmakers employed the narrative form to tell stories and show comic incidents. An early narrative film was *L'Arroseur*
10 *arrosé (The Waterer Watered),* made in 1895 by the French Lumière Brothers. Today's big budget, special effects movies have their roots in these early days of filmmaking. The French filmmaker Georges Méliès, who was also a magician, devel-
15 oped a technique for showing magical transformations in his films. His 1902 film *Le Voyage dans la Lune (A Trip to the Moon)* shows a rocket ship landing on the "man in the moon's" face.
20 Let's look at some highlights starting from these early days of moviemaking up to the Hollywood of today.

Scene from Le Voyage dans la Lune (A Trip to the Moon)

Early Cinema 1893–1903

1893—Thomas Alva Edison builds the world's
25 first movie studio in West Orange, New Jersey.

1895—The Lumière Brothers hold one of the first public showings of motion pictures projected on a screen at the Grand Café in Paris.

A Lumière Brothers advertising poster

Classical Hollywood Cinema (pre-sound) 1903–1927

1903—American director Edwin S. Porter makes *The Great Train Robbery,* the prototype for the classical American film.

1910—Eastern (U.S.) film companies move permanently to California because of the good weather and the diverse locales (such as mountains, deserts, and beaches).

1910s to 1920s—Small movie studios merge to create the large Hollywood firms that still exist today such as Fox, MGM, and Paramount.

A poster for The Great Train Robbery

German Expressionism 1919–1926

1920—The film *The Cabinet of Dr. Caligari* done in the German artistic style, expressionism, is a big success in Europe and the United States. In it, images are distorted and exaggerated to show the viewpoint of a madman.

1922—The expressionist horror film, *Nosferatu,* based on the story of Dracula, appears. The style of this film later influences many American horror classics such as *The Son of Frankenstein* (1939).

French Impressionism and Surrealism 1918–1930

1918 to 1928—The French filmmaking styles, impressionism and surrealism, appear.

A scene from Nosferatu

Impressionist films deal with the character's inner actions, such as thoughts, dreams, and fantasies. Surrealist films show the unconscious mind. They are anti-narrative and illogical, as in dreams.

1922—French filmmaker Abel Gance makes *La Roue (The Wheel)*, a five-hour impressionist film about four characters' feelings for each other.

1928—The surrealist film *Un Chien Andalou (An Andalusian Dog)* appears. In it, a woman locks a man in a room and then turns around to find him inexplicably behind her. In one scene, ants appear to crawl out of a human hand.

Classical Hollywood Cinema (post-sound) 1926–1959

1927—The first Hollywood film with sound, *The Jazz Singer,* is a tremendous success.

1935—The first color films appear (*Becky Sharp,* 1935 and *The Trail of the Lonesome Pine,* 1936) using a technology called Technicolor.

1950s—New cinematic technologies appear: 3-D, widescreen, and stereo sound. Television causes audiences to become smaller.

Italian Neorealism and French New Wave 1942–1964

1940s—Post World War II Italian film-making develops a realistic film style called neorealism. Neorealist films show contemporary, realistic social conditions. An example is Roberto Rossellini's *Open City* (1945), about a group of people who fight against the Nazis.

1950s—A new generation of filmmakers in France rebels against the French filmmaking establishment. At the same time, they pay homage to the classical Hollywood movie. This movement is called "New Wave." New Wave cinematographers use new filming techniques such as the long shot and the hand-held camera. An example of French New Wave is Jean-Luc Godard's *A Bout de Souffle (Breathless)*.

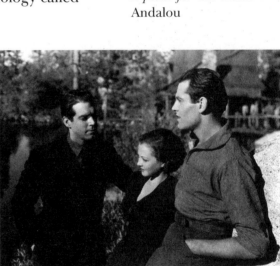

A poster for Un Chien Andalou

A scene from The Trail of Lonesome Pine, *one of the first color films*

The New Hollywood and Independent Filmmaking 1960s–Present

95

1969—Hollywood companies are losing over 200 million dollars annually because audiences are getting smaller and television companies are making their own (cheaper) movies.

100

1970s to 1980s—New, young filmmakers such as George Lucas (*Star Wars*), Steven Spielberg (*E.T.*), and Martin Scorsese (*Taxi Driver*) are winning recognition.
At this time, there are relatively few minority film directors in Hollywood.

105

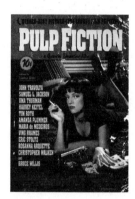

A scene from A Bout de Souffle (Breathless)

1990s—Independent films such as *Pulp Fiction* (1994) and *The Sixth Sense* (1999) experiment with narrative construction via flashbacks and other tricks to disrupt the logical flow of time in the story.

110

A poster for Pulp Fiction

2000s—The final episodes of *Star Wars* are released.

Word Count: 735

Source: *Film Art: An Introduction* (Bordwell and Thompson)

Timed Reading

Read "Film History Timeline: 1893 to the Present" again. Read at a comfortable speed. Time your reading. Write your time in the Timed Reading Chart on page 234.

Start time: _____

End time: _____

My reading time: _____

Comprehension

1. What are the seven major periods in the history of filmmaking from the 1800s to the present?

   _____   _____

   _____   _____

   _____   _____

   _____

2. Describe in your own words what the first films were like.

   _____

   _____

3. Why did many American film companies move to California?

   _____

   _____

4. What film is an example of German expressionism? Why is it an example?

   _____

   _____

5. What film is an example of French surrealism? Why is it an example?

   _____

   _____

6. List five cinematic technologies that were invented between 1926 and 1959.

   _____   _____

   _____   _____

   _____

Talk About It

Talk about the movies mentioned in the timeline. Have you seen them? What are some recent technologies in moviemaking?

Have you seen *Star Wars?*

I . . .

Reading 2: The New Hollywood

Before You Read

Reading Skills

Using Topic Sentences to Preview

You've already seen how to preview a passage by reading the introductory and the concluding paragraphs. You can also preview by looking at the body paragraphs, the middle paragraphs of a reading. Body paragraphs usually have topic sentences that tell you the main idea of the paragraph. If you read all the topic sentences, you can get a pretty good idea of the main ideas of the passage. Note that topic sentences are often—but not always—the first sentence in a body paragraph.

Look at the first sentence of the fifth paragraph of "Ethics in Business: Hewlett-Packard" on page 83 of Chapter 4:

HP is also concerned with social and environmental responsibility.

What can you expect to read about in this paragraph? ➤ Examples of how Hewlett-Packard shows that it is concerned about people and the environment.

Practice

A. Preview "The New Hollywood" on pages 107–109. Read and underline the first sentence of Paragraphs 2, 3, 4, 5, 6, 7, 8, 9, and 10.

B. Now write what you think each paragraph is about. Compare your answers with a partner's answers.

Paragraph 2: _____

Paragraph 3: _____

Paragraph 4: _____

Paragraph 5: _____

Paragraph 6: _____

Paragraph 7: _____

Paragraph 8: _____

Paragraph 9: _____

Paragraph 10: _____

Preview

A. The title of Reading 2 is "The New Hollywood." You read a little about the New Hollywood on page 103, and you previewed the topic sentences in the reading. What information about the New Hollywood might this reading contain? Which directors or types of movies might it describe? Discuss your ideas with a partner.

B. Preview these words and expressions from Reading 2. Circle *T* (True) or *F* (False). If you are not sure, guess.

1. **Aesthetics** is the study of artistic value or beauty.   T   F

2. A movie that is similar to another one or is based on other people's work is considered **innovative**.   T   F

3. You can describe a movie with a lot of action and exaggerated characters as **understated**.   T   F

4. Experimental, creative directors often have the quality of **ingenuity**.   T   F

5. A **conventional** movie is one that is very different from other movies.   T   F

6. **Divisiveness** is another word for "agreement."   T   F

7. A mystery is a kind of movie that has a lot of **intrigue**.   T   F

8. You can say that a movie that is **stunningly photographed** is beautiful to look at.   T   F

C. Preview these moviemaking expressions from Reading 2. Match each expression with the correct definition. Write the letter of the correct answer on the line.

Expressions	Definitions
_____ **1.** a critical success	**a.** a movie that makes a lot of money
_____ **2.** commercially distributed	**b.** how the story is organized in a movie
_____ **3.** a financial success	**c.** a movie that the critics liked
_____ **4.** narrative structure	**d.** when all the scenes in a movie are logical and well connected
_____ **5.** tight editing	**e.** a movie that is shown in theaters to paying customers

As You Read

As you read, think about this question:
▶ What are the main characteristics of the "New Hollywood," the Hollywood from the 1970s to the present?

🎧 The New Hollywood

In the era of classical Hollywood movies, studios made huge profits. By the 1960s, the industry began to lose money, particularly on big-budget pictures. However, the later part of the 20th century saw big changes in the movie industry.

1970s—A New Generation of Directors

5   During the 1970s, a new generation of talented moviemakers— among them Francis Ford Coppola, Brian de Palma, George Lucas, Martin Scorsese, and Steven Spielberg—brought fresh energy to Hollywood. Most of them had studied film history, aesthetics, and production as academic subjects in graduate programs in Los Angeles
10 and New York. And all of them shared a love of both old Hollywood movies and innovative European and Japanese cinema.

Director George Lucas

Their directing styles tended to mix the conventional with the experimental. Their work showed great ingenuity and creativity. They didn't reject the classic Hollywood style; rather they added their
15 own stylistic ideas to conventional moviemaking. Most of their movies showed strong narrative structure, clear characterizations, careful camera work, tight editing techniques, and a superb command of dramatic action.

These young moviemakers initially enjoyed extraordinary independence and creative freedom. Critics began to discuss the beginning of a "new Hollywood" domi-
20 nated by directors rather than studio bosses. Some of the film-school educated directors themselves seemed to think they were in charge. "The studios are corporations now, and the men who run them are bureaucrats," said George Lucas. "They know as much about making movies as a banker does. . . But the real power lies with us—the ones who actually know how to make movies."

25 1990s—Directorial Diversity

By the 1990s, the movie industry had become more open to diverse directorial talent. Unlike in the old studio era, many minority group members became successful directors. For example, during the 1990s, nearly two dozen black directors were at work on a wide range of movie projects. Some, like Julie Dash, the first African-

American woman to direct a commercially distributed feature film, specialized in personal pictures. Her quiet turn-of-the-century tale *Daughters of the Dust* (1991) focuses on the female descendants of slaves living on the Sea Islands of Georgia. Others have worked in more popular cinematic genres (forms). Carl Franklin, for example, excelled in neo-*noir*, a modern version of the 1940s and 1950s film *noir* genre, crime stories without happy endings. Some of his work includes the highly atmospheric *Devil in a Blue Dress* (1995), starring Denzel Washington as an African-American private eye in post-World War II Los Angeles.

A scene from Devil in a Blue Dress

Asian-American directors like Ang Lee, who first achieved acclaim with understated movies such as *Sense and Sensibility* (1995) and *The Ice Storm* (1997), have also been successful in Hollywood. To direct *Crouching Tiger, Hidden Dragon* (2000), featuring Chow Yun-Fat (*Anna and the King*, 1999), Michelle Yeoh (*Tomorrow Never Dies*, 1997), and Zhang Ziyi, one of Beijing's major young stars, the Taiwan-born Lee returned to his roots in China. Filmed in Mandarin and released in the West with subtitles, this highly choreographed martial arts movie was both a critical and a financial success.

Hong Kong filmmaker Jackie Chan also found regular work in the American movie industry, although more as a comedic actor than as a director. A big star in Asia, Chan finally found success in Hollywood in 1996 with *Rumble in the Bronx*. After that, the engaging martial arts expert starred in such hit movies as *Rush Hour* (1998), *Shanghai Noon* (2000), and *Rush Hour 2* (2001).

Directors from Bollywood, the center of Indian filmmaking in Bombay, also had an impact on American cinema. Bombay filmmaker Shekhar Kapur, for instance, directed *Elizabeth* (1998), a stunningly photographed epic of intrigue and divisiveness within the sixteenth-century British court. It was nominated for seven Academy Awards, including an Oscar for best picture.

A poster for Crouching Tiger, Hidden Dragon

Women moviemakers in general have found success in Hollywood in recent years. Some female directors have dealt with distinctly "women's subjects." Examples include Amy Heckerling's satire on upper-class teen culture, *Clueless* (1995), based on Jane Austen's *Emma*; Karyn Kusama's *Girlfight*, about a female boxer (2000), and Joan

Chen's romance tale *Autumn in New York* (2000). Others have made films that are less easy to categorize. Kathryn Bigelow, for example, directed *Strange Days* (1995), a dazzling but uneasy mix of socially relevant
75 issues and futuristic action. Writer-director Mary Harron's movies include *American Psycho* (2000), a deliciously evil, perversely amusing look at the mind of a serial killer (Christian Bale) who seems to have stepped off the pages of *GQ* magazine. It contains
80 moments of extreme violence that could repulse even the greatest horror film fan.

A scene from Rush Hour

Despite this increased diversity, directing in Hollywood was still dominated by white males at the beginning of the 21st century. In the 1980s, the number of women directing theatrical movies went from zero to
85 about 7 or 8 percent of the total. Over the next decade, however, those figures remained about the same. According to a 1998 study by the Directors Guild of America, female directors worked fewer than 5 percent of the total days Guild members spent on theatrical movies in 1997—a 50 percent decline from the prior year. Although female membership in the Guild has risen to about 2,000 of the 11,000
90 total members, no more than 10 percent of the major movies made in any given year are made by women. As a recent article notes, this situation persists despite the fact that several studios are run by women. The lack of a major African American presence among Hollywood directors is also noticeable, despite the existence of the Directors Guild of America's African-American Steering Committee, founded in 1994.

Word Count: 930

Source: *Making Sense of Movies: Filmmaking in the Hollywood Style* (Stanley)

Timed Reading

Read "The New Hollywood" again. Read at a comfortable speed. Time your reading. Write your time in the Timed Reading Chart on page 234.

Start time: _____

End time: _____

My reading time: _____

After You Read

Main Idea

What are the main characteristics of the "New Hollywood"?

_____

_____

_____

Getting the Details

Answer the following questions. Use complete sentences.

1. Give two examples of how the new generation of directors in the 1970s was different from previous generations of moviemakers.

_____

_____

2. Give three examples of the following statement from the reading: "By the 1990s, the movie industry had become more open to diverse directorial talent."

_____

_____

_____

3. In what way is *Devil in a Blue Dress* an example of a "more popular cinematic genre"?

_____

_____

4. Does the author feel that there is enough diversity in Hollywood today? How can you tell? Paraphrase the lines in the reading that support your inference.

_____

_____

_____

Reading Skills

Identifying Facts and Opinions

When you read, it's important to know the difference between facts and opinions. A fact is an idea that has evidence. It can be proven. An opinion cannot be proven. For example, look at this sentence from "Ethics in Business: Hewlett-Packard" in Chapter 4:

> HP was founded in 1939 by William Hewlett and David Packard.

Is this a fact or an opinion? It's a fact because you can verify it many ways, such as looking it up in a book about the history of the company. Now look at this statement from the same reading:

> One company that is exemplary in its commitment to ethical behavior and its model ethical guidelines is the high-technology company Hewlett-Packard (HP).

Is it a fact or an opinion? You can't prove how committed HP is. It's the author's opinion that HP is a good example of a company that is committed to ethical behavior.

Practice

Read each of the following statements from "The New Hollywood." Decide if it expresses a fact or an opinion, if it can be verified or not. Check (✓) the correct box.

Statements	Fact	Opinion
1. During the 1970s, a new generation of talented moviemakers—among them Francis Ford Coppola, Brian de Palma, George Lucas, Martin Scorsese, and Steven Spielberg—brought fresh energy to Hollywood.		
2. For example, during the 1990s, nearly two dozen black directors were at work on a wide range of movie projects.		
3. In the 1980s, the number of women directing theatrical movies went from zero to about 7 or 8 percent of the total.		
4. Most of their movies showed strong narrative structure, clear characterizations, careful camera work, tight editing techniques, and a superb command of dramatic action.		
5. Filmed in Mandarin and released in the West with subtitles, this highly choreographed martial arts movie was both a critical and a financial success.		

Vocabulary

A. Here are some more words from "The New Hollywood." Find them in the reading and circle them.

Noun	Verb	Adjectives	Adverb
satire	repulse	atmospheric dazzling	perversely

B. Now use them to complete the sentences.

1. *Fargo* is a(n) _____ funny movie because the characters are both funny and evil.

2. *Titanic* is a(n) _____ movie. The glittering costumes and colorful sets are spectacularly beautiful.

3. Violence in movies can _____ some people; in fact, sensitive viewers often look away during violent scenes.

4. *Chicago* is a(n) _____. It's a humorous but insulting view of the American legal system.

5. What often makes film noir movies _____ is that the black and white photography creates a sense of mystery.

Talk About It

Discuss these questions.

1. What is the most recent film that you saw? Who made it? What country was it made in?
2. If someone made a movie of your life, who should play you? Who should direct it? Which actors should play the important people in your life?
3. Have you seen any of the films mentioned in "The New Hollywood"? If so, which ones? What did you think of them?

What is the most recent film . . . ?

I saw . . .

Expressions

Collocations for Discussing Film History

Collocations are words that are frequently used together. Here are some collocations from the two readings in this chapter. They relate to film history.

achieved acclaim with
consisted of (a single shot)
found success in (Hollywood)
have their/his/her roots in (the early days)
led to (a series of discoveries)
pays homage to (the classical Hollywood movie)
rebel against (the establishment)
returned to his roots in (China)

Notes: These collocations are verb phrases. Pay particular attention to the prepositions in these collocations. It's a good idea to memorize them.

Examples:
The invention of photography **led to** a series of discoveries.
The Taiwan-born Lee **returned to his roots in** China.

Practice

A. Find and underline the collocations from the box above in "Film History Timeline: 1893 to the Present" and "The New Hollywood." As you underline them, pay particular attention to the prepositions in these collocations. Try to memorize them.

B. Now use some of them to complete the sentences. There may be more than one correct answer for some items.

1. The African-American director F. Gary Gray _____ his remake of *The Italian Job* in 2003 because it was both a critical and box office success.

2. *Devil in a Blue Dress* _____ the film *noir* genre of the 1940s and 1950s by using some of the characteristics of those films.

3. The 2001 movie *Waking Life* by Richard Linklater _____ animated scenes. There were no live action scenes in the movie.

4. Many modern horror films _____ the German expressionist classic, *Nosferatu*. Although it's old, it continues to inspire modern filmmaking.

5. Shekhar Kapur is a Bollywood director who _____ Hollywood with his movie *Elizabeth*.

Learning about Film History on the Internet

You can find a lot of information about movies and movie directors on the Internet. One of the best ways is to use a movie database such as the Internet Movie Database (**www.imdb.com**). You can also do keyword searches using a search engine (such as **www.google.com**). You can search for information on film styles (such as *New Wave*), director's names (such as *Carl Franklin*), movie titles (such as *Le Voyage dans la Lune*), and actor's names (such as *Denzel Washington*).

You can get very specific, targeted information by combining these terms. For example, if you type *"Carl Franklin" and "Denzel Washington"* into the Google search box, you will get information about films that the director and the actor worked on together.

Note: You don't have to capitalize proper nouns in a search engine.

Practice

Practice finding film history information on the Internet. Find out about any aspect of film history that interests you or about the following aspects of film history:

▶ German expressionist film directors, movies, or actors

▶ Italian neorealist film directors, movies, or actors

▶ French surrealist, impressionist, or New Wave film directors, movies, or actors

▶ New Hollywood film directors, movies, or actors

▶ Minority film directors, movies, or actors

▶ Silent films

Share your search experience with the class. On what topic did you do your search? Why did you choose this topic? What keywords did you use? What did you learn that you didn't know before you did your search?

Write About It

Write about film history. Choose one of these topics:

▶ Describe your first—or your best—movie-going experience: What did you see? Where did you see it? Who did you see it with? What were your impressions of the entire experience?

▶ Write about the topic that you researched in your Internet search.

Use five words and expressions from this chapter. Also, try to use your Internet research.

On Your Own

Project

Interview classmates on their favorite classic movie.

Step 1: Practice

Write five interview questions designed to find out some of your classmates' favorite classic movies. Write them in the box below. Try to get some or all of the following information:

- ▶ the name of the movie
- ▶ when it was made
- ▶ the director
- ▶ the actors

- ▶ the type of movie it is
- ▶ their opinion of the movie
- ▶ if or how the movie influenced them

After you write your questions, practice them with a partner and have your teacher help you pronounce them correctly.

Interview Questions

1. _____
2. _____
3. _____
4. _____
5. _____

Step 2: Conduct the Interview

Ask classmates about their favorite classic movie. You may want to take notes. You'll give your results to the class later.

Step 3: Follow-Up

Explain the results of your interview to the class.

Wrap Up

How Much Do You Remember?

Check your new knowledge. In this chapter you learned facts, words, and expressions. You also learned reading skills and you practiced writing. Complete the following to check what you remember.

1. Give an example of a German expressionist film. _____

_____

_____

2. Give two examples of diversity in the "New Hollywood." _____

_____

_____

3. Why is it a good idea to look at the topic sentences of a passage before you read it? _____

_____

4. Use *narrative* in a sentence. _____

_____

5. Use *pay homage to* in a sentence. _____

_____

6. Explain one way to find film history information on the Internet. _____

_____

_____

Second Timed Readings

Now reread "Film History Timeline: 1893 to the Present" and "The New Hollywood." Time each reading separately. Write your times in the Timed Reading Chart on page 234.

Crossword Puzzle

Complete the crossword puzzle to practice some words and expressions from this chapter.

Clues

Across ➡

1. Very beautiful to look at
6. Another word for *model*
7. If a movie is a _____ success, the critics liked it.
10. The study of beauty
11. A humorous way to criticize someone or something

Down ⬇

1. Interrupt
2. Combine
3. Directors such as Steven Spielberg _____ _____ to classical Hollywood movies.
4. Some modern horror movies have their _____ in classics from the early days such as *Nosferatu*.
5. Predictable or unadventurous
8. Mystery
9. Julie Dash is one of the African American directors who have achieved _____ in the New Hollywood.

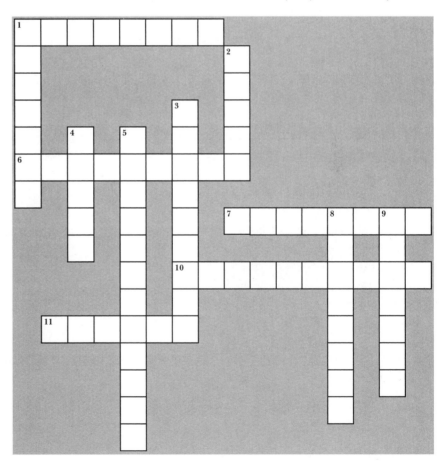

 **6 Genre Films**

CHAPTER PREVIEW

In this chapter, you'll:

Content
► read a review of the movie *Star Wars*
► learn the characteristics of specific film types, or film genres

Reading Skills
► combine previewing skills
► identify similarities and differences in a reading

Vocabulary Skills
► use words and expressions for talking about genre films
► use adjective collocations for describing genre films

Writing Skills
► write a movie review

Internet Skills
► find movie reviews on the Internet

> A long time ago in a galaxy far, far away... ☙
>
> — *The opening lines of* Star Wars

SHORT SURVEY

I like movies that make me:
❑ laugh
❑ cry
❑ tense
❑ scared
❑ think
❑ other: _____

Reading 1:

Why do critics consider *Star Wars* an important movie? Read Roger Ebert's *Star Wars* review to find out.

Reading 2:

What are the significant characteristics of different movie genres? Find out in "Genre Films."

What do you think?

Answer the questions in the box. Compare your answers with a partner.

Movies and Me

1. **What are your favorite film genres? Check (✓)** *Like* **or** *Don't Like* **below.**

	Like	Don't Like
adventure	☐	☐
comedy	☐	☐
horror	☐	☐
kung fu	☐	☐
musical	☐	☐
thriller	☐	☐
science fiction	☐	☐
Western	☐	☐

2. **What are your four favorite movies?**

_____   _____

_____   _____

3. **Why do you like these movies?** _____

_____

_____

4. **Are they all the same genre?** _____

5. **Who are your favorite actors (male or female)?** _____

   Why do you like these actors? _____

Reading 1: A Review of Star Wars

Before You Read

Preview

A. The title of Reading 1 is "A Review of *Star Wars*." What kind of information does a movie review usually include? Discuss your ideas with a partner.

> A movie should have a beginning, a middle, and an end, though not necessarily in that order. 🐚
>
> — *Jean-Luc Godard (French movie director, b. 1930)*

B. How important are movies to you? Circle the answer(s) that apply to you. Compare and discuss your answers with a partner.

1. **When I want to choose a movie to see, I _____.**

   a. read a review in my school newspaper

   b. read a review in the city newspaper

   c. look for reviews on the Internet

   d. ask friends

2. **What is most important to you in a movie review?**

   a. whether the reviewer liked the movie or not

   b. who the actors are

   c. who the director is

   d. the plot (story)

   e. how long the movie is

3. **I will see any movie my friends want to see.**

   Agree   Disagree

4. **I sometimes go to movies on a school night.**

   Agree   Disagree

5. **I like to talk about movies with my friends.**

   Agree   Disagree

6. **I could be a good movie reviewer. I can describe a movie without telling too much—just enough so others want to see it.**

   Agree   Disagree

Vocabulary

Here are some words from "A Review of *Star Wars*." Match each word with its correct definition. Write the letter of the correct answer on the line.

Words

_____ **1.** fastidious

_____ **2.** deceptively

_____ **3.** hovers over

_____ **4.** inspirations

_____ **5.** melded

_____ **6.** to pan

_____ **7.** a quest

_____ **8.** watershed

Definitions

a. blended; put together

b. in a misleading way

c. a critical point; a turning point

d. a search or journey to find something

e. hangs in the air; flies or is suspended over

f. neat; paying careful attention to detail

g. creative ideas, ones that usually occur suddenly

h. to move a camera back and forth over a scene or landscape

A scene from Star Wars

As You Read

As you read, think about this question:

▶ Why is *Star Wars* such an important movie?

🎧 A Review of *Star Wars*

Roger Ebert is a film reviewer for the *Chicago Sun-Times.* He reviewed the science fiction/fantasy film *Star Wars* when it first came out and then reviewed it again
5 20 years later. Here is an adaptation of that review, published in his book *The Great Movies.*

To see *Star Wars* again after 20 years is to revisit a place in the mind. George Lucas' space
10 epic has completely become part of our memories. It's a masterpiece. Those who analyze its philosophy do so, I imagine, with a smile in their minds. May the Force be with them.

Star Wars was a technical watershed that influenced many of the movies that came after. *Star Wars* melded a new generation of special effects with the high-energy action picture; it linked
15 space opera and soap opera, fairy tales and legend, and packaged them as a wild visual ride.

It's a good-hearted film in every single frame, and shining through is the gift of a man who knew how to link state-of-the-art technology with a deceptively simple, really very powerful story.

Two Lucas inspirations started the story with a tease: He set the action not in the future
20 but "long ago," and jumped into the middle of it with "Chapter 4: A New Hope." These seemingly innocent touches were actually rather powerful; they gave the saga the aura of an ancient tale, and an ongoing one.

As if those two shocks were not enough for the movie's first moments, I learn from a review by Mark R. Leeper that this was the first film to pan the camera across a star field:
25 "Space scenes had always been done with a fixed camera, and for a very good reason. It was more economical not to create a background of stars large enough to pan through." As the camera tilts up, a vast spaceship appears from the top of the screen and moves overhead, an effect reinforced by the surround sound. It is such a dramatic opening that it's no wonder Lucas paid a fine and resigned from the Directors Guild rather than obey its demand that
30 he begin with conventional opening credits.

The film has simple, well-defined characters, beginning with the robots C-3PO (fastidious, a little effete) and R2-D2 (childlike, easily hurt). The evil Empire has all but triumphed in the galaxy, but rebel forces are preparing an assault on the Death Star. Princess Leia (pert, sassy Carrie Fisher) has information pinpointing the Death Star's vulnerable point and feeds it into

35 R2-D2's computer; when her ship is captured, the robots escape from the Death Star and find themselves on Luke Skywalker's planet, where soon Luke (Mark Hamill as an idealistic youngster) meets the wise, old, mysterious Obi-Wan Kenobi (Alec Guinness) and they hire the freelance space jockey Han Solo (Harrison Ford, already laconic) to carry them to Leia's rescue.

Many of the planetscapes are startlingly beautiful, and owe something to fantasy artist

40 Chesley Bonestell's imaginary drawings of other worlds. The final assault on the Death Star, when the fighter rockets speed between parallel walls, is a nod in the direction of *2001: A Space Odyssey*, with its light trip into another dimension: Kubrick showed, and Lucas learned, how to make the audience feel it is hurtling headlong through space.

Lucas fills his screen with loving touches. Luke's weather-worn "Speeder" vehicle, which

45 hovers over the sand, reminds me uncannily of a 1965 Mustang. And consider the details creating the presence, look, and sound of Darth Vader, whose fanged facemask, black cape, and hollow breathing are the setting for James Earl Jones' cold voice of doom.

Seeing the film the first time, I was swept away and have remained swept ever since.

The film philosophies that will live forever are the simplest-seeming ones. They may have

50 profound depths, but their surfaces are as clear to an audience as a beloved old story—*The Odyssey, Don Quixote, David Copperfield, Huckleberry Finn*—which are all same: A brave but flawed hero, a quest, colorful people and places, sidekicks, the discovery of life's underlying truths. If I were asked to say which movies will still be widely known a century from now, I would list *2001: A Space Odyssey,* and *The Wizard of Oz,* and probably *Casablanca. . .*

55 and *Star Wars,* for sure.

Word Count: 728

Source: *The Great Movies* (Ebert)

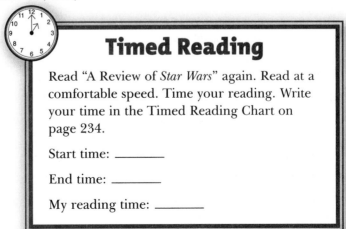

Timed Reading

Read "A Review of *Star Wars*" again. Read at a comfortable speed. Time your reading. Write your time in the Timed Reading Chart on page 234.

Start time: _____

End time: _____

My reading time: _____

After You Read

Comprehension

1. Why is *Star Wars* an important movie?

   _____

   _____

   _____

   _____

2. According to Roger Ebert, George Lucas had two inspirations. What were they?

   _____

   _____

   _____

   _____

3. What unusual way did Lucas use the camera in the opening of *Star Wars?*

   _____

   _____

   _____

   _____

4. Ebert says that the film has "simple, well-defined characters." How does he characterize R2-D2, Luke, and Obi-Wan Kenobi?

   _____

   _____

   _____

   _____

5. What kinds of film philosophies does Ebert say will last forever?

_____

_____

_____

_____

6. Explain in your own words the theme (main idea) of stories such as *The Odyssey* and *Star Wars:*

_____

_____

_____

_____

Talk About It

Discuss these questions.

1. If you have seen *Star Wars*, what is your opinion of the movie? If not, does the review make you want to see the movie? Why or why not?
2. Do you like science fiction/fantasy movies?
3. What kinds of characters usually appear in most science fiction/fantasy movies? If you can, give examples.

Reading 2: Genre Films

Before You Read

Reading Skills

Putting It All Together to Preview

In previous chapters, you used titles, headings, introductions and conclusions, and topic sentences to preview a reading. Together, these strategies are powerful previewing tools. You can combine all or some of these skills. Practice combining previewing skills whenever you start a new reading.

Practice

Answer the following questions to practice combining previewing skills.

1. What is the title of Reading 2 (page 128)? _____

   What do you think it will be about? _____

2. Read the introduction. What background information is in the introduction?

   _____

   _____

3. Read the five headings in Reading 2 and write what you think each section might be about.

   Section 1: _____

   _____

   Section 2: _____

   _____

   Section 3: _____

   _____

   Section 4: _____

   _____

   Section 5: _____

   _____

4. Read and underline the first sentence of Paragraphs 1, 3, and 8. Then write what you think each paragraph is about.

Paragraph 1: _____

_____

Paragraph 3: _____

_____

Paragraph 8: _____

_____

5. Look at the pictures and read the captions. Why do you think these pictures are here? What do

they tell you? _____

Preview

A. The title of Reading 2 is "Genre Films." You read a little about the science fiction genre on pages 122 and 123, and you used your previewing skills to prepare. What information about genres films do you expect to find in Reading 2? Discuss a few examples with a partner.

B. Preview these words from the reading. Match each word with the correct definition. Write the letter of the correct answer on the line.

<u>Words</u>

_____ **1.** anarchy

_____ **2.** assume

_____ **3.** gutter

_____ **4.** reaffirmed

_____ **5.** resolution

_____ **6.** setting

_____ **7.** shorthand

<u>Definitions</u>

a. confirmed again; gave support to

b. a state of lawlessness; confusion, disorder

c. where a film takes place

d. believe without having knowledge of the facts

e. place between the curb and the street that carries rain water

f. a quick way of writing or explaining something

g. what happens at the end of a story, closure

As You Read

As you read, think about these questions:
▶ What can you expect to find in a western movie?
  What can you expect in a gangster movie?

🎧 Genre Films

Genre films are film stories that are repeated again and again
with only slight variations. They follow the same basic pattern and
include the same basic ingredients. Genre films include Westerns,
gangster movies, film noir, war stories, horror pictures, science
5   fiction or fantasy films, screwball romantic comedies, and musi-
cals. These genres were so popular—and therefore so profitable
for the movie studios—that they made them over and over again.

*Western film star
John Wayne*

The Strengths of Genre Films

By the time of the first talking movie, 1927, the main genres for movies were
10 established. Film noir became popular in the 1940s
and science fiction movies came in during the 1950s.
For the director, there were certain advantages to
working within a given genre. Because the characters, the plot, and the conventions were already
15 established, they provided the director with a kind of
cinematic shorthand that greatly simplified the task
of storytelling.

The genre film simplifies film watching as well as
filmmaking. In a Western, because of the conven-

A science fiction movie poster

20 tions of appearance, dress, manners, and typecasting, we recognize the hero, the
sidekick, or the villain on sight and assume they will not violate our expectation of
their conventional roles. Our familiarity with the genre makes watching not only
easier but in some ways more enjoyable. Because we know and are familiar with

all the conventions, we gain pleasure from recognizing each character, each image, each familiar situation.

Basic Genre Conventions

The five basic conventions of a genre are setting, characters, conflict, resolution, and values reaffirmed. We will look at some of these for two genres.

The Western

In a Western, the actions take place in the American West or Southwest, west of the Mississippi River, usually at the edge of the frontier. The time span is between 1865 and 1900.

The hero is a rugged individualist, often a mysterious loner. He is very much his own man and acts in accordance with his personal code, not in response to community pressures or for personal gain. His personal code emphasizes human dignity, courage, justice, fair play, equality (the rights of the underdog), and respect for women. He is intelligent, resourceful, kind, honest, firm, and consistent in his dealings with others. Even-tempered and peaceable by nature, he does not seek violent solutions but responds with violent action when the situation demands it. He is quick and accurate with a pistol, good at riding a horse, and strong in a barroom brawl.

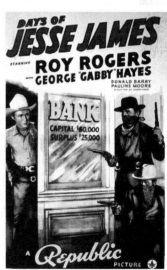

This movie poster shows the convention in Westerns of the hero wearing a white hat and the villain wearing a black hat.

There are two categories of villain. The first includes outlaws who bully, threaten, and generally terrorize the respectable citizens of the frontier community. They try to take what they want by force: stealing cattle, robbing banks or stages, or attacking stagecoaches, wagon trains, or ranches. Villains in the second category work under the guise of respectability: crooked bankers, saloon owners, and sheriffs or wealthy ranchers, all motivated by greed for wealth or lust for power.

Some villains are killed in gunfights. Others are frightened off or imprisoned. Once he takes care of the villain and society is in decent, just, and capable hands, the hero is free to move on.

Another convention of westerns is the way heroes and villains look. The hero wears a white or light-colored hat. He is clean-cut and clean-shaven. Villains wear black hats and mustaches. Sidekicks and villains may have beards, but sidekicks' beards are gray and uncombed, and villains' beards are black and well groomed.

With westerns, there are also conventions of action. Most westerns have one or more of the following: a shootout between the hero and villain in the town's only street or among the rocks of a canyon, a prolonged chase on horseback (usually accompanied by shooting), and a knock-down, drag-out barroom brawl (and a scared bartender periodically ducking behind the bar).

At least one convention is structural. Many westerns begin with the hero riding into view from the left side of the screen and end with him riding off in the opposite direction, usually into a fading sunset.

The Gangster Film

The classic gangster film usually takes place among the many streets and crowded buildings in the older part of the modern city. Much of the action occurs at night, and rain is often used to add atmosphere. In the rural gangster film, the action takes place in a rural setting with small towns, cheap restaurants, and gas stations.

The poster for The Roaring Twenties

The gangster hero is a brutal, aggressive, lone-wolf type. He is cocky and ambitious, the self-made man who fought his way up from nothing and had a lot of trouble in his life.

Women, generally, are symbols of the hero's status. They are cheap, mindless, and greedy, fascinated by the hero's cruelty and power. Sometimes a decent intelligent woman associates with the hero early in the film but soon discovers his true nature and abandons him. The gangster's mother and sister are civilized and social women with traditional values. The mother is respected; the sister protected.

The conflict in gangster movies is the anarchy of the gangsters versus the social order. Because the police represent the social order, the conflict also involves cops versus robbers. There is usually a conflict of robbers versus robbers, with the struggle involving leadership of the gang or a territorial rights gang war 90 against a rival mob. There is also often an internal conflict within the hero, in which his latent good or social instincts struggle against his essentially cruel and selfish nature.

The classic gangster "hero" achieves success temporarily but eventually meets his deserved end. Although he may be given a chance for reform and redemp- 95 tion, the criminal side of his nature is too strong to be denied. He often dies in the gutter, in a cowardly, weak manner. His dignity and strength are gone—everything we admired about him is destroyed. The other gang members are either killed or jailed, and the social order is restored.

In the gangster genre, good conquers evil, or evil destroys itself. Crime does 100 not pay. Civilized values of human decency, honesty, and respect for law and order are reaffirmed.

A Final Note

People enjoy genre films because they know what to expect, and the genre films meet their expectations.

Word Count: 1,026

Source: *The Art of Watching Films* (Boggs and Petrie)

Timed Reading

Read "Genre Films" again. Read at a comfortable speed. Time your reading. Write your time in the Timed Reading Chart on page 234.

Start time: _____

End time: _____

My reading time: _____

Good movies make you care, make you believe in possibilities again. ✍

— *Pauline Kael (American film critic, 1919–2001)*

After You Read

Main Idea

Write a statement that expresses the main idea of "Genre Films."

_____

_____

Getting the Details

Answer the following questions.

1. Eight kinds of genre films were listed in the reading. What are six of them?

_____   _____

_____   _____

_____   _____

2. How does genre film simplify film watching? _____

_____

_____

_____

3. What are the five conventions of a genre? _____

_____

_____

_____

4. What is one structural convention of Westerns? _____

_____

5. In your own words, describe the conflicts in a gangster movie. _____

_____

_____

Reading Skills

Noting Similarities and Differences

Good readers take notice of similarities and differences as they read. Professors often give exams or writing assignments in which students must compare or contrast information from readings or lectures. Therefore, it makes sense to go back to a reading and make notes on any similarities or differences expressed about certain aspects of the topic.

One way to do this is to create a graphic organizer. This allows you to quickly see similarities and differences. It also can help you remember information because you have categorized it and written it down. (Note: When you take notes in a comparison graphic organizer, avoid using complete sentences; paraphrase and use abbreviations instead.)

For example, if you were going to compare horror movies and science fiction movies, your graphic organizer might look like this:

	Horror Films	Science Fiction Films
Setting	dark house	outer space
Characters	weak, innocent, young girl; strong, brave, young man; alien life form	smart, brave, young girl; strong, brave, young man; alien life form
Conflict	good and evil	good and evil

Practice

Read "Genre Films" again. Make a graphic organizer like the one below. Use it to take notes on similarities and differences. If there is no information on a convention, leave that box empty. Compare your graphic organizer with a partner's.

	Western Films	Gangster Films
Setting		
Female Characters		
Male Characters		
Clothing		
Conflict		
Resolution		

Vocabulary

A. Here are some more words from "Genre Films." Find them in the reading and circle them.

Nouns	Verb	Adjectives
a. redemption b. underdog	c. bully	d. cocky e. crooked

B. Now match each word in the box with the highlighted words or expressions in the sentences. Write the letter of the correct answer on the line.

_____ **1.** At the end of the movie, the villain is given a chance for **becoming a better person**.

_____ **2.** The bankers and gamblers in many gangster films are **dishonest**.

_____ **3.** Norm was very **sure of himself** and never thought he could be wrong.

_____ **4.** Gary was the **one that everyone expected to lose**.

_____ **5.** Richard would **be mean to** children smaller than he was.

Talk About It

Discuss these questions.

1. What are some typical scenes that you would find in a science fiction, film *noir*, horror, romantic comedy, adventure, or war movie?

2. What was the last movie you saw? Which genre was it? Did you like it? Why or why not? What is the next movie you are planning to see? Why?

3. What makes you like a movie? What makes you dislike a movie?

What are some typical scenes in a horror movie?

In horror movies . . .

Expressions

Adjective Collocations for Discussing Genre Films

Collocations are words that are frequently used together. Here are some adjective + noun collocations from the two readings in the chapter. They relate to film genres.

fading sunset	personal code
fixed camera	rugged individualist
knock-down, drag-out barroom brawl	space opera*
latent instincts	soap opera*
(be his) own man	surround sound*
prolonged chase	vulnerable point

* *Space* and *soap* are nouns used as adjectives. *Surround* is a verb used as an adjective.

Examples:
The hero rode off on the right side of the screen into the **fading sunset**.
Surround sound reinforced the effect of the big spaceship flying in space.

Practice

A. Find and underline the collocations in the box above in "A Review of *Star Wars*" and "Genre Films."

B. Now use some of them to complete the sentences.

1. A _____ is one form of action audiences like in Westerns. In fact, fans expect to see a long chase scene.

2. Ned, the Western hero, was his _____ and had his own

   _____. He did what he thought was right and did not listen to others.

3. In a typical _____, you learn more and more each day about the troubles that a set of characters have. In the past, soap companies paid for all the advertising on these shows.

4. Finding the Death Star's weakness or _____ allows the heroes of *Star Wars* to succeed.

5. In the earlier movies, the space scenes were done with a _____, a camera that did not move.

6. Eddy's hidden good qualities made him an appealing hero. These _____ made his struggle with his own character believable.

Internet Research

Finding Movie Reviews on the Internet

You can easily find movie reviews on the Internet. Using quotation marks, type in *review* and the name of the movie into a search engine such as **www.google.com**. For example, if you type *review star wars* without the quotation marks, you will get about 6,000,000 results. With the quotation marks, you get about 7,000 results. If you know a critic you like, add his or her name. For example, with *ebert* + *"star wars review"* you will get about 54 results.

You can also find reviews in newspaper and magazine websites such as *The New York Times, Time*, and *Newsweek*. Online magazines such as *Slate* also have reviews. From the homepage of a newspaper or magazine, look for links such as Entertainment, Reviews, and Arts and Life to find movie reviews.

Note: With most search engines, you don't need to use small words like *of* and you don't need to capitalize proper nouns.

Practice

Practice finding movie reviews on the Internet. Follow these steps:

1. Do a search for a review of your favorite movie. Find one and bring the review to class.
2. Choose a current movie and see if Roger Ebert has a review of it. If he does, bring the review to class.
3. Find two or three reviews of any movie you are interested in and bring them to class. Tell the class about the similarities and differences of the reviews.

Write About It

Write a film review. Follow these steps:

1. Read the reviews you found on the Internet again.
2. Analyze the format of the review. What do the writers do first, next, and so on? How do the reviews end? How much of the story do they tell? How do they comment on setting, character, conflict, and resolution? Make an outline based on your analysis.
3. Using your outline, write a review of one of your favorite movies, or see a movie you haven't seen before and write a review of it.

Use five words and expressions from this chapter. Also, try to use your Internet research.

On Your Own

Project

Give an oral presentation of a movie review.

Step 1: Prepare

Watch or listen to a movie review on the radio, TV, or the Internet. As you are watching or listening, think about these questions: How do oral movie reviews begin and end? How much information is given?

Next, with a partner (if possible) choose a movie to review and watch it. Take notes on the director, actors, and writer. Take notes on the content and anything that seems especially interesting or surprising. Think about how you will organize your review. Make notes for your oral presentation.

Step 2: Give the Presentation

Present your review to the class. If you saw the movie with a classmate, present the movie together. You might want to start your review by saying "thumbs up" (meaning the movie was good) or "thumbs down" meaning the movie was bad.

Step 3: Follow-Up

Discuss your presentations. Did any of your classmates' reviews influence you? Why? Which movies do you plan to see? Which do you plan to avoid?

Federico Fellini's La Dolce Vita

> Talking about dreams is like talking about movies, since the cinema uses the language of dreams; years can pass in a second and you can hop from one place to another. It's a language made of image. And in the real cinema, every object and every light means something, as in a dream. ❧
>
> — *Frederico Fellini (Italian filmmaker, 1920–1993)*

Wrap Up

How Much Do You Remember?

Check your new knowledge. In this chapter you learned facts, words, and expressions. You also learned reading skills and you practiced writing. Complete the following to check what you remember.

1. Give one reason that George Lucas's masterpiece *Star Wars* is a technical watershed. _____

_____

2. What are two of the major film genres? _____

_____

3. Give one characteristic for each of these genres: Westerns and gangster movies. _____

_____

_____

4. What is one way to record the similarities and differences in a reading? _____

_____

_____

5. Use *deserved* in a sentence. _____

6. Use *assume* in a sentence. _____

7. How do you find movie reviews on an online newspaper or magazine website? _____

_____

_____

Second Timed Readings

Now reread "A Review of *Star Wars*" and "Genre Films." Time each reading separately. Write your times in the Timed Reading Chart on page 234.

Crossword Puzzle

Complete the crossword puzzle to practice some words and expressions from this chapter.

Clues

Across →
2. Dishonest
3. Sure of him- or herself
4. Be rough and unkind to
7. Blended together
10. Creative ideas
12. A person who is expected to lose

Down ↓
1. A long chase
5. Hidden character traits
6. In a misleading way
8. Weakness
9. A camera that doesn't move
11. A daily TV show, usually about families and their problems

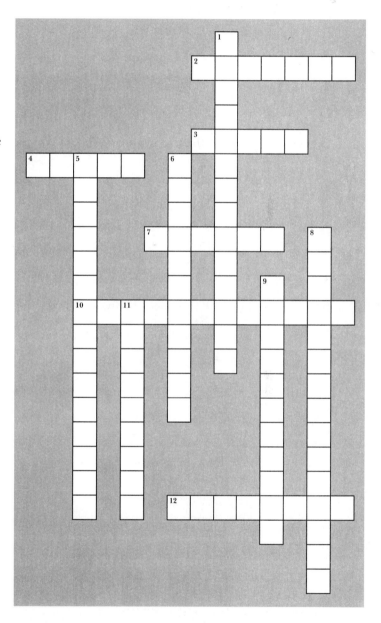

What is Human Geography?

Human geography looks at people and how they interact with the land on which they live. It involves the study of small towns as well as big cities—anywhere that people live. Human geography includes population geography, environmental geography, and economic geography. Other areas in human geography include:

- cultural geography
- human environment interaction
- political geography
- historical geography
- urban geography

The Greek scholar Eratosthenes (276–194 B.C.), who measured the circumference of the Earth and was the first to use the word "geography," is commonly called the father of geography.

SOME FAMOUS HUMAN GEOGRAPHERS

Paul Vidal de la Blache—French; studied people's effect on the environment, 1845–1918

Ellen Churchill Semple—American; studied environmental determinism, 1863–1932

Carl Sauer—American; studied cultural landscapes, 1889–1975

Torsten Hagerstrand—Swedish; studied space and time's effects on the environment, 1916–2004

Peter Haggett—British; studied the spread of diseases in human populations, 1933–

Human Geography and You

The study of human geography is helpful in careers such as environmental planning; urban design; cartography (mapmaking); consulting; and research in government, academic, or industrial settings.

Do you want to study human geography? Ask yourself these questions:

- Am I curious about how people interact with their environment?
- Do I like to do research?
- Am I interested in cultures?

CHAPTER 7 Population

CHAPTER PREVIEW

In this chapter, you'll:

Content
▶ read about population trends
▶ learn about immigration patterns in several countries

Reading Skills
▶ use pictures and captions to preview a reading
▶ use graphic organizers to record information in a reading

Vocabulary Skills
▶ use words and expressions to discuss population and population trends
▶ use collocations to describe population issues

Writing Skills
▶ describe an immigration experience
▶ describe your experiences with population growth

Internet Skills
▶ find recent population statistics on the Internet

> Children are one third of our population and all of our future. ❧
>
> — *Select Panel for the Promotion of Child Health, 1981*

SHORT SURVEY

The growing world population is:

❑ a great problem

❑ somewhat of a problem

❑ not a problem

❑ a good thing

❑ neutral (neither good nor bad)

❑ other: _____

Reading 1:
What is happening to world population? Read "Population Trends" to find out.

Reading 2:
Which countries have growing immigrant populations? Find out in "Nations of Immigrants."

What do you think?

Answer the questions in the box. Compare your answers with a partner.

Immigration Patterns and You

1. Where do you live? How long have you lived there? Where did you move from?

_____

_____

2. Did your grandparents live in the same place their whole lives? Explain.

_____

_____

3. Do any people in your neighborhood speak more than one language? How long have they lived in

the neighborhood? _____

_____

4. Do you live in a place that is crowded? Is the population increasing or decreasing where you live?

How do you feel about this? _____

_____

_____

5. How do social, political, or economic issues in your community affect the population in your area? For example, is there enough housing for the people who want to live there?

_____

_____

Reading 1: Population Trends

Before You Read

Preview

A. The title of Reading 1 is "Population Trends." What kind of information might it include? What do you know about the population trends in the place where you live now? Discuss your ideas with a partner.

B. How much do you already know about population trends? Circle *T* (True) or *F* (False).

1. The world's population grows about 77 million each year.   T   F

2. In 2004, there were 6.4 billion people on Earth.   T   F

3. In 2050, there will probably be about 7.4 billion people.   T   F

4. In 2100, there will be fewer people in Europe than today.   T   F

5. In less developed countries, the population will increase   T   F
by about 60 percent between 2000 and 2050.

6. In 2002, the Prime Minister of Singapore asked for zero   T   F
population growth (a population growth rate of zero).

C. Several factors make up population data. Match each factor with the correct definition. Write the letter of the correct answer on the line.

Factors	Definitions
_____ **1.** density of settlement	**a.** the number or percent of men and women
_____ **2.** fertility	**b.** the number of people in an area of land
_____ **3.** mortality	**c.** birthrate; having children; reproduction
_____ **4.** sex distribution	**d.** death

Vocabulary

A. Here are some words and expressions from "Population Trends." Match each word or expression in the oval with the correct definition. Write the letter of the correct answer on the line.

> a. anticipated   c. estimated   e. population projections   g. reversal
> b. conceal   d. interpretation   f. potential   h. trend

_____ **1.** the direction of a change; a tendency

_____ **2.** a change in the opposite direction

_____ **3.** future possibility

_____ **4.** guessed at

_____ **5.** predictions about future numbers of people

_____ **6.** hide

_____ **7.** expected

_____ **8.** an explanation of something that is not immediately obvious

B. Look at the graphs below. With a partner, try to explain the difference between *population trends* and *growth trends*.

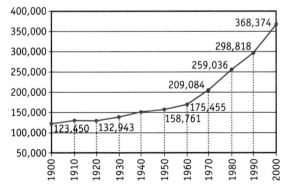

Population trends in Springfield, Massachusetts

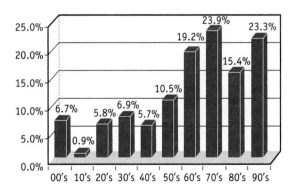

Growth trends in Springfield, Massachusetts

As you read, think about this question:
▶ What are the most recent population trends?

🎧 Population Trends

In 1972, the Prime Minister of Singapore asked for zero or even negative population growth. The people of Singapore responded so well that by the mid-1980s, the birth rates were below the level needed to replace the
5 population. He then had to tell the people of Singapore to have more children, "At least two. Better three. Four if you can afford it." The policy reversal in Singapore reflects a population reality: The numbers and distributions of people not yet born are being determined now.
10 Furthermore, the size characteristics, along with the growth trends and migrations of today's populations are features that help shape the well being of people not yet born.

We look at seven aspects of population data—the numbers, age, and sex distribution of people; patterns and trends in their fertility and mortality; their density
15 of settlement, and rate of growth—because they affect the social, political, and economic organization of a society. In addition, all of these are affected by the social, political, and economic organization of a society, as the Singapore example shows. Through population data, we begin to understand how people in a given area live, how they may interact with one another, how they use the land, what
20 pressure on resources exists, and what the future may bring.

Some Population Patterns

In the 13 years between 1991 and 2004, the Earth's population grew from nearly 5.4 billion people to 6.4 billion people. That means that the world population grew about 77 million people annually, or 211,000 people per day. The
25 average, however, conceals the reality that annual increases have been declining over the years. In the early 1990s, the reported yearly growth was 85 million. Even with the slower pace of estimated increase, the United Nations early this century still projected that the world would likely contain nearly 9 billion inhabitants by 2050 and 9.5 billion inhabitants by 2100. It is hard to imagine what these
30 large numbers mean, but some statistics may help you understand. You had lived

a *million* seconds when you were 11.6 days old. You won't be a billion seconds old until you are 31.7 years of age.

The Value of Diagrams

In learning about population trends, reading a text can provide you with a lot of information; often, however, you can understand (and really see) the same amount of information more easily by reading a graph or diagram. The following diagrams explain some world population patterns. Of course, diagrams often need interpretation to explain the data fully and prevent misinterpretation.

Let's look at world population numbers and projections. The numbers tell us about the population today, and the projections tell us about the population in the future.

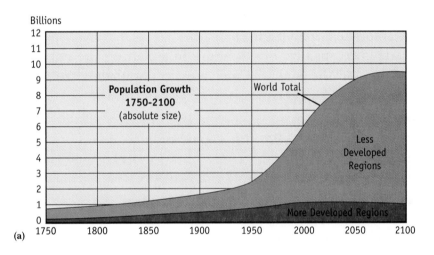

(a)

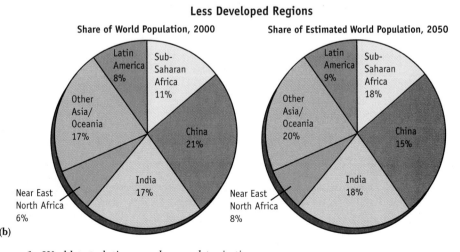

(b)

Figure 1: *World population numbers and projections*

Let's take a look at Figure 1a. After two centuries of slow growth, world population began explosive expansion following World War II. United Nations demographers project a global population of nearly 9 billion in 2050. Declining growth
45 rates in much of the developing world have lowered earlier estimates of global population for the year 2100 from 10 billion to no more than 9.5 billion: some demographers argue for reducing it further to between 8 and 9 billion. Numbers in more developed regions at mid-century will be the same or lower than at its start, thanks to anticipated population loss in Europe. However, higher fertility
50 rates and immigration are projected to increase U.S. population by nearly 45% between 2000 and 2050, and large volume immigration into Europe could alter its population decline projections. In contrast, the populations of the less developed regions may increase by almost 60% between 2000 and 2050.

Figure 1b shows the changes in population for less developed regions between
55 2000 (left diagram) and 2050 (right diagram).

These charts give a picture of the future in a glance. The implications of the present numbers and the potential increases in population are of vital current social, political, and ecological concern.

Word Count: 667

Source: *Human Geography* (Fellmann, Getis, Getis, and Malinowski)

Timed Reading

Read "Population Trends" again. Read at a comfortable speed. Time your reading. Write your time in the Timed Reading Chart on page 235.

Start time: _____

End time: _____

My reading time: _____

After You Read

Comprehension

1. What are the most recent population trends? _____

_____

2. What was the result of the Prime Minister of Singapore's request for zero or even negative population growth?

_____

_____

3. What are the seven aspects of population data? _____

_____

_____

4. What happened to the Earth's population between 1991 and 2004?

_____

_____

5. If annual population increases have been declining each year, why is the Earth's population growing?

_____

_____

Talk About It

Discuss these questions.
1. What consequences do you see around you of the increases in population?
2. What can we understand through the study of population data?

Reading 2: Nations of Immigrants

Before You Read

Reading Skills

Using Pictures and Captions to Preview

Photographs, diagrams, drawings, and other images help you to understand ideas in a reading. Authors use captions (headings and/or explanations underneath images) to give you additional information. If you look at images and their captions *before* you read, they can help you to predict what the reading is about. If you look at the pictures and captions *as* you read, they will help you understand the author's ideas. Pictures and captions can also help you understand new words.

It's important to look at pictures and read their captions because instructors sometimes ask about that information on quizzes and exams.

Practice

Look at the figures and captions in "Nations of Immigrants" on pages 152–155 and answer the following questions.

1. Look at the caption for Figure 1. What does this figure show? _____

   _____

2. Look at Figure 2. What two points does it make?_____

   _____

3. Look at Figure 3. What percentage of people were born outside of these countries?

   a. Switzerland _____

   b. France _____

   c. the United States _____

   d. Sweden _____

   e. Germany _____

Preview

A. The title of Reading 2 is "Nations of Immigrants." You read a little about population trends on pages 146–148, and you read the captions and looked at the figures. What information do you think that "Nations of Immigrants" will contain? Which countries might it describe? Discuss your ideas with a partner.

B. Preview these words from the reading. Match each word with the correct definition. Write the letter of the correct answer on the line.

Words	Definitions
_____ **1.** colonists	**a.** consist of; be composed of
_____ **2.** comprise	**b.** throws out; pushes out
_____ **3.** descent	**c.** control
_____ **4.** disparities	**d.** ancestry; origin
_____ **5.** domination	**e.** differences
_____ **6.** ejects	**f.** to stop; to hold back; to decrease
_____ **7.** famines	**g.** shortages of food leading to hunger and starvation
_____ **8.** to stem	**h.** people who come to a new land to live

C. Preview more words from the reading. Circle *T* (True) or *F* (False).

1. A "**melting pot**" country is one in which different cultures do not mix together well.   T   F

2. **Indigenous** populations are people who move to a new country.   T   F

3. **Post-communist** Eastern Europe is the time before the communists ruled in Eastern Europe.   T   F

4. To **accelerate** is to go slower and slower.   T   F

5. Countries who give political **asylum** give people protection so they can live in a place where they will be safe.   T   F

6. **Amerindians** are American Indians.   T   F

As You Read

As you read, think about this question:
▶ What are some nations with large immigrant populations?

🎧 Nations of Immigrants

Americans have a belief in a "melting pot" myth and heritage. They are inclined to forget that many other countries are also "nations of immigrants" and that their numbers are dra-
5 matically increasing. In the United States, Canada, Australia, and New Zealand, early colonists from Europe, and later, immigrants from other continents, overwhelmed indigenous populations. In each country, immigra-
10 tion has continued contributing not only to national ethnic mixes but maintaining or enlarging the proportion of the population that is foreign born. In Australia, as one exam-

The Statue of Liberty

ple, that population now equals 25%; in Canada, it is 18%.

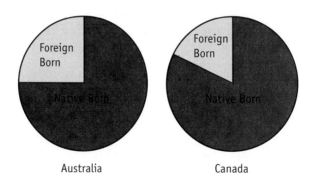

Figure 1: *A comparison of the native populations of Australia and Canada*

15 In Latin America, the domination of native people by Europeans was and is less complete and uniform than in Anglo-America. In nearly all South and Central American states, European and other nonnative ethnic groups dominate the social and economic hierarchy. In many countries, however, they constitute

only a minority of the total population. In Paraguay, for example, the vast majority of inhabitants are native Paraguayans who pride themselves on their Native
American descent, and Amerindians comprise nearly half of the populations of
Peru, Bolivia, and Ecuador. But European ethnics make up over 90% of the population of Argentina, Uruguay, Costa Rica, and southern Chile, and about 50% of
the inhabitants of Brazil.

Countries where nearly 50% of the population is of Native-American descent	Countries where over 90% of the population is of European descent
Bolivia Ecuador Peru	Argentina Costa Rica Southern Chile Uruguay

Figure 2: *Comparison of ethnic populations in Latin-American countries*

The original homelands of these European immigrant groups are themselves
increasingly becoming multiethnic, and several of these European countries are
now home to proportionally as many or more peo-
ple born outside of Europe as there are people born
outside the United States living in the U.S. About
20% of Switzerland's population, 13% of France's,
10% of Sweden's, and over 9% of Germany's are
people born outside of those countries, compared
with America's 12%. See Figure 3 on page 154.

Many came as immigrants and refugees fleeing
unrest or poverty in post-communist Eastern
Europe. Many are "guest workers" and their families who were earlier recruited in Turkey and
North Africa, or they are immigrants from former
colonial or overseas territories in Asia, Africa, and
the Caribbean. More than 7% of Germany's inhabitants come from outside the European Union, as
do 3% of Holland's and Belgium's.

Map of Latin America

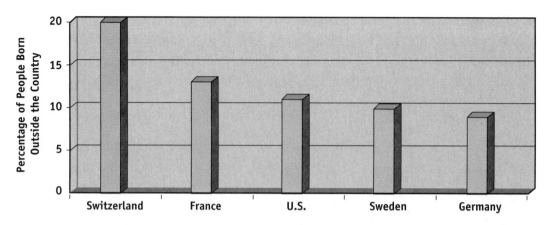

Figure 3: *Comparison of percent of people born outside the country living in the U.S. and European countries*

The trend of ethnic mixing is certain to continue and accelerate. Cross-border movements of migrants and refugees in Africa, Asia, the Americas, as well as in Europe, are continuing common occurrences, reflecting growing incidences of ethnic strife, civil wars, famines, and economic hardships. But of even greater long-term influence are the growing disparities in population numbers and economic wealth between the older developed states and the developing world. The population of the world's poorer countries is growing twice as fast as Europe's of the late 19th century, when massive groups of immigrants moved to North America. The current rich world, whose population is projected to stabilize well below 1.5 billion, will increasingly be a magnet for those from poorer countries where numbers will rise about 4 billion to reach a number which will probably be more than 6.5 billion by 2025 A.D. and to nearly 8 billion in a half-century. The economic and population pressures building in the developing worlds insure greater international and inter-continental migration and a rapid expansion in the numbers of "nations of immigrants."

Many of those developed host countries are beginning to resist that flow. Although the Universal Declaration of Human Rights declares that individuals are to be free to move within or to leave their own countries, there is no guaranteed admittance to other countries. Political asylum is often—but not necessarily—granted. Refugees or migrants seeking economic opportunity or fleeing civil strife or starvation have no claims for acceptance. Increasingly, they are being turned away. The Interior Minister of France advocates "zero immigration" and Germany's government closed its doors in 1993 by increasing border controls and changing its constitutional right to asylum. Britain in 1994 tightened immigration rules even for foreign students and casual workers. And all European Union countries—which have no common EU policies on illegal immigration—have measures for turning back refugees who come via another EU country. In 1995, the EU's members narrowed the definition of who may qualify for asylum. Additional individual and collective restrictions have been enforced during the later 1990s and into the 21st century.

Nor is Europe alone. Hong Kong ejects Vietnamese refugees; the Congo orders Rwandans to return to their own country; India tries to stem the influx of Bangladeshis; the United States rejects "economic refugees" from Haiti. Algerians are increasingly resented in France as their numbers and cultural presence increase. Turks feel the enmity of a small but violent group of Germans, and East Indians and Africans find growing resistance among the Dutch. In many countries, policies of exclusion or restriction appear motivated by unacceptable influences of specific racial, ethnic, or national groups.

Word Count: 988

Source: *Human Geography* (Fellmann, Getis, Getis, and Malinowski)

Timed Reading

Read "Nations of Immigrants" again. Read at a comfortable speed. Time your reading. Write your time in the Timed Reading Chart on page 235.

Start time: _____

End time: _____

My reading time: _____

After You Read

Main Idea
What are some nations with large immigrant populations?

_____

Getting the Details
Answer the following questions. Use complete sentences.

1. What are the main English-speaking countries with large immigrant populations?

_____

_____

2. Where are cross-border movements of migrants and refugees continuing common occurrences?

_____

_____

3. Immigrants and refugees leave because of difficulties in their home countries. What are some of these difficulties?

_____

_____

4. What does the Universal Declaration of Human Rights say about the freedom of individuals to move within or leave their own countries?

_____

_____

5. Do all countries welcome immigrants? Support your answer with examples from the reading.

_____

_____

_____

_____

Reading Skills

Using Your Own Graphic Organizer to Take Notes

As you have seen, photographs, diagrams, and drawings help you to understand ideas in a reading. It is often useful to make your own diagrams—or graphic organizers—to help you understand and remember what you read. You can use the graphic organizers that you've seen in previous chapters, or you can design your own. For example, in "Population Trends," you saw a line graph and two pie graphs. Other types of graphs include bar graphs such as the ones on pages 145 and 154.

You can organize information any way that makes sense to you. For example, "Nations of Immigrants" talked about the number of Amerindians in Peru, Bolivia, and Ecuador and the number of European ethnics in Argentina, Uruguay, Costa Rica, and southern Chile. To remember these numbers, you can draw a map of South America and use two kinds of shadings to show the differences or write the numbers on the map itself.

Practice

Use "Nations of Immigrants" on pages 152–155 to make graphic organizers on a separate piece of paper to show the following information.

1. Draw a graphic organizer to show the difference between the numbers of immigrants in Australia and Canada.

2. Use a map of Europe to show the following: "About 20% of Switzerland's populations, 13% of France's, 10% of Sweden's, and over 9% of Germany's are people born outside those countries."

3. Use a graphic organizer to explain the following: "The current rich world is projected to stabilize below 1.5 billion. Poorer countries' numbers will probably be more than 6.5 billion."

Vocabulary

A. Here are some more words from "Nations of Immigrants." Find them in the reading and circle them.

Nouns	Verbs	Adjective
enmity	overwhelmed	collective
incidences	recruited	

B. Now use them to complete the sentences.

1. More workers were needed, so guest workers were _____ from Turkey and North Africa. They were invited to immigrate to Europe.

2. The early colonists _____ the indigenous populations. Because they were over-powered, the indigenous populations decreased in number.

3. Some countries had _____ restrictions, which meant that groups of people (for example, Haitians) were not allowed to enter those countries.

4. There were a number of _____ of fighting. These cases of strife pushed residents to become immigrants and leave their homelands.

5. The two ethnic groups did not like each other. This _____ made them uncomfortable around each other.

Talk About It

Discuss these questions.

1. What surprised you most in the "Nations of Immigrants" reading?

2. How important do you think issues of immigration are in the place where you live?

3. Should people who have no criminal record be free to move to any other country? Why or why not?

Expressions

Collocations for Discussing Population Issues

Collocations are words that are frequently used together. Here are some collocations from the two readings in this chapter. They relate to population and immigration.

affected by	**policies on immigration**
(be) a magnet for	**rate of growth**
distributions of people	**right of admittance**
policies of exclusion	

Note: These collocations all have prepositions.

Examples:

All of these are **affected by** the social, political, and economical organization of a society.

The rich world will increasingly **be a magnet for** those from poorer countries.

Practice

A. Find and underline the collocations in the box above in "Population Trends" and "Nations of Immigrants." As you underline them, pay particular attention to the prepositions in these collocations. Try to memorize them.

B. Now use them to complete the sentences.

1. The _____ indicates the speed at which something is increasing.

2. A country's _____ determine how many people it will let in each year.

3. The _____ are policies that prevent people from entering a country.

4. California _____ immigrants because there are so many opportunities to work on farms.

5. Everyone is _____ the increasing world population because countries are interdependent.

6. It is interesting to look at the _____ in a country. Usually there are more people on the coasts than in the interior of a country.

7. There is no _____. In other words, you cannot move to any country you want.

Internet Research

Learning about Recent Population Statistics on the Internet

You can find a lot of information about population and immigration on the Internet.

For population statistics about the United States, the United States census website is a good source: **www.census.gov/**.

The United States government also keeps statistics on the world population: **www.census.gov/ipc/www/world.html**.

Another source is the nonprofit organization the Population Reference Bureau: **www.prb.org/**.

Because population and immigration trends can change rapidly, the Internet is a good source of up-to-date information.

Practice

Practice finding population and immigration information on the Internet. Find out about any aspect of population and immigration information that interests you or about the following:

▶ the projected population of the world in 20, 50, and 100 years

▶ recent population statistics for a country of your choice

▶ immigration patterns 1920–1950

▶ immigration patterns 1950–1990

▶ recent immigration patterns

Share your search experience with the class. On what topic did you do your search? Why did you choose this topic? What keywords did you use? What did you learn that you didn't know about before? If you found interesting photos, diagrams, or graphs, bring them to class.

Write About It

Write about population and immigration. Choose one of these topics:

▶ Describe how you feel about population growth. How does it affect you personally? Do you feel more crowded than you did three years ago? Where do you feel crowded/ not crowded? Does your school have more students? What is your experience?

▶ Write about an immigration experience of your own or someone you know.

Use five words and expressions from this chapter. Also, try to use your Internet research.

On Your Own

Project

Prepare a presentation on population or immigration.

Step 1: Prepare

Work in groups. First, decide on the topic you want to present. Brainstorm all the topics that interest the group. Then vote for your top three and decide on one. You may wish to choose one of your Internet research topics or one of the following:

- ▶ interview recent immigrants about their experience
- ▶ interview classmates about their feelings about population growth
- ▶ look at the population growth in your city, state, or country
- ▶ interview classmates about how many children they are planning to have
- ▶ (other) _____

Decide how to share the work: who will do which parts of the research, who will conduct which interviews, and how everyone will present the findings.

Look for information about your topic in books or magazine and newspaper articles, or on the Internet and take notes. Look for or create charts, graphs, or diagrams to help present your information.

If you are conducting an interview, write your interview questions. Practice your presentation with your group members. Have your teacher help you pronounce new words and collocations that you want to use.

Step 2: Give the Presentation

Give your presentation to the class. Take turns speaking. Make eye contact with (look into the eyes of) your audience. The audience should take notes and ask questions afterwards.

Step 3: Follow-Up

Discuss your presentations. Which were interesting? What made them interesting? What will you do differently the next time that you give a presentation?

Wrap Up

How Much Do You Remember?

Check your new knowledge. In this chapter you learned facts, words, and expressions. You also learned reading skills and you practiced writing. Complete the following to check what you remember.

1. Explain the Prime Minister of Singapore's 1972 policy and why he needed to change it. _____

   _____

   _____

2. Give four examples of what is included in population data. _____

   _____

   _____

3. What is the value of images and captions in a reading? _____

   _____

   _____

4. Use *affected by* in a sentence. _____

   _____

5. Use *disparities* in a sentence. _____

   _____

6. Explain one way to find population information on the Internet. _____

   _____

   _____

Second Timed Readings

Now reread "Population Trends" and "Nations of Immigrants." Time each reading separately. Write your times in the Timed Reading Chart on page 235.

Crossword Puzzle

Complete the crossword puzzle to practice some words and expressions from this chapter.

CLUES

Across ➡

2. Policies of _____ are policies about people coming into a country.
6. Possible
8. Influenced by
12. Stop; decrease
13. A change in the opposite direction

Down ↓

1. Expected
3. Go faster
4. Differences
5. Push out
7. A safe place to live

9. Times when there is too little food and people starve
10. Settlers in a new country
11. Hide

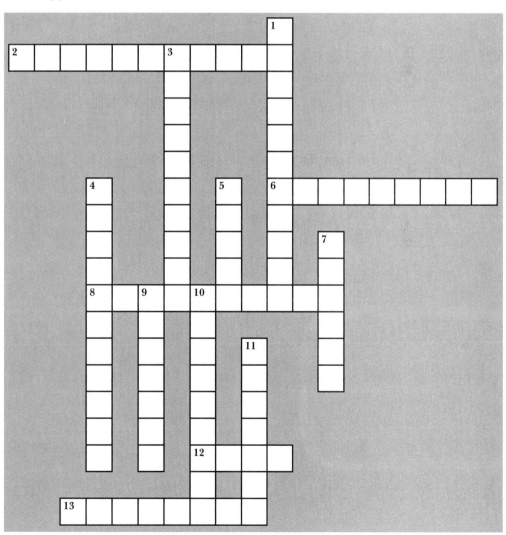

CHAPTER 8 People and the Environment

CHAPTER PREVIEW

In this chapter, you'll:

Content
▶ find out what happened to Easter Island
▶ learn how humans have affected the environment for thousands of years

Reading Skills
▶ have an open mind as you approach new material
▶ identify causes and effects

Vocabulary Skills
▶ use words and expressions to describe the environment
▶ use collocations to discuss human effects on the environment

Writing Skills
▶ explain what you are doing to help improve the environment

Internet Skills
▶ identify unbiased information on the Internet

> The history of life on earth has been a history of interaction between living things and their surroundings. 🐚
>
> — *Rachel Carson (American writer and environmentalist, 1907–1964)*

SHORT SURVEY

I am _____ concerned about the environment.

❏ extremely

❏ very

❏ somewhat

❏ slightly

❏ not at all

❏ other: _____

Reading 1:

Why did the Polynesian society on Easter Island disappear? "The Mystery of Easter Island" suggests a possible answer.

Reading 2:

What effects do human cultures have on the environment? Read "Cultural Ecology" to find out.

What do you think?

Express your opinions on the environment by answering the questions in the box. Compare and discuss your opinions with a partner.

The Environment and You

1. The greatest problem in the world today is _____.

    a. poverty   **c.** the environment   **e.** overpopulation   **g.** hunger
    b. war   **d.** disease   **f.** other: _____

2. The worst environmental problem is _____.

    a. disappearing plant and animal species   **c.** pollution
    b. global warming   **d.** other: _____

3. My concern for the environment extends to _____.

    a. my home   **c.** my neighborhood   **e.** my community
    b. my region   **d.** my country   **f.** the entire planet

4. Humans are to blame for environmental problems such as pollution and endangered plant and animal species.

                  Agree   Disagree

5. The main cause of environmental damage is _____.

    a. overpopulation   **b.** technology   **c.** other: _____

6. Modern societies have caused more environmental problems than societies in the past.

                  Agree   Disagree

7. In the past, people knew how to live in harmony with nature.

                  Agree   Disagree

8. I think it is impossible to correct environmental problems at this point.

                  Agree   Disagree

Now discuss with your partner: Can any environmental problems be corrected? If so, what are some of the solutions?

Reading 1: The Mystery of Easter Island

Before You Read

Preview

A. The title of Reading 1 is "The Mystery of Easter Island." What do you already know about Easter Island? What do the picture and map on page 168 tell you about Easter Island? What do you think this reading is about? Discuss your ideas with a partner.

B. Check your knowledge and assumptions about Polynesian cultures and environments. Discuss your answers to the following questions with a partner.

1. What are the names of some Polynesian or Pacific islands?

2. What kind of weather do you typically find in Polynesia?

3. What does the landscape look like?

4. What kinds of plants grow there? What kinds of food do people eat?

5. Have you ever spent time on a Polynesian or Pacific island? Which one(s)?

6. Do you think that life was easy or hard on a Polynesian island in the past? Today?

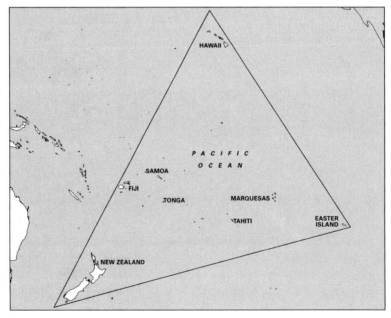

Map of Polynesia

Vocabulary

Here are some words from "The Mystery of Easter Island." Match them with the highlighted words or expressions in the sentences. Write the letter of the correct answer on the line.

a. deforestation   c. enhanced   e. leeched   g. quarries   i. timber
b. desolate   d. habitable   f. massive   h. sediment   j. wasteland

_____ **1.** Today, the island is **deserted**. No one lives there anymore.

_____ **2.** Scientists sometimes study the **layers of earth** for ancient plant and animal life. This substance can tell them a lot about what lived in a place many centuries ago.

_____ **3.** Societies need **wood** for fuel and housing.

_____ **4.** Today, the island is a **place where no one lives and nothing can grow**.

_____ **5.** Too much rain **removed** all the nutrients in the ground; now nothing can grow.

_____ **6.** The island used to be **livable**; now no one can live there.

_____ **7.** The **removal of all the trees** caused serious problems. As a result, there was no fuel or wood for houses.

_____ **8.** A visit to Hawaii **increased** Sam's understanding of the island lifestyle.

_____ **9.** Easter Island is famous for its **enormous** statues.

_____ **10.** The researchers found several **pits or deep holes in the ground filled with large stones** where they assumed that the statues were built.

> The first law of ecology is that everything is related to everything else. 🐚
>
> — *Barry Commoner (American biologist and environmentalist, b. 1917)*

As you read, think about this question:
▶ What happened to the ancient Polynesians who lived on Easter Island?

🎧 The Mystery of Easter Island

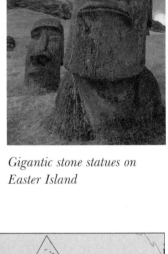

Gigantic stone statues on Easter Island

Among the greatest mysteries of human history are those of vanished civilizations. Everyone who has seen the abandoned buildings of ancient civilizations such as the Khmer (in Cambodia), the Maya (in Mexico), or the
5 Anasazi (in the southwestern United States) immediately asks the same question: Why did the societies that erected those impressive structures disappear?

Among all such vanished civilizations, that of the former Polynesian society on Easter
10 Island remains the most mysterious. The mystery stems primarily from the island's gigantic stone statues and its desolate landscape, and it is enhanced because to so many people, Polynesia represents the magic of the
15 ultimate in exotic romance. In other words, Polynesia symbolizes paradise.

Easter Island, only 64 square miles, is the world's most isolated scrap of habitable land. It lies in the Pacific Ocean more than 2,000
20 miles (1,200 kilometers) west of South America, 1,400 miles (840 kilometers) from even the nearest habitable island, Pitcairn. Its subtropical location helps give it a rather mild climate, while its volcanic origins make its soil fertile.

Map of Polynesia

25 The island gets its name from its discovery by the Dutch explorer Jacob Roggeveen, on Easter (April 5) in 1722. Roggeveen's first impression was not of a paradise but of a wasteland. The island Roggeveen saw was grassland without a single tree or bush over ten feet high. The islanders Roggeveen encountered had no source of real firewood to warm themselves during Easter Island's cool,

wet, windy winters. Their native animals included nothing larger than insects. For domestic animals, they had only chickens.

Easter Island's most famous feature is its huge stone statues, more than 200 of which once stood on massive stone platforms lining the coast. At least 700 more, in all stages of completion, were abandoned in quarries or on ancient roads between the quarries and the coast. Most of the erected statues were carved in a single quarry and then somehow transported as far as six miles (3.6 kilometers)—despite heights as great as 33 feet (10.5 meters) and weights up to 82 tons (74,389 kilos). The abandoned statues, meanwhile, were as much as 65 feet tall and weighed up to 270 tons (244,910 kilos).

Roggeveen himself quickly recognized the problem the statues posed: "The stone images at first caused us to be struck with astonishment," he wrote, "because we could not comprehend how it was possible that these people, who are devoid of (didn't have) heavy, thick timber for making any machines, as well as strong ropes, nevertheless had been able to erect such images."

The statues imply a society very different from the one Roggeveen saw in 1722. The number and size of the statues suggest a population much larger than the 2,000 people he encountered. What became of everyone? Furthermore, that society must have been highly organized. What happened to that organization, and how did it even arise in such a barren landscape in the first place? Is it possible that this barren landscape could have once supported the trees necessary to construct the statues?

The last question can be answered by the scientific research technique of pollen analysis, which involves analyzing samples of layers of sediment from a pond. The most recent deposits are at the top of the sample, and the relatively more ancient deposits are at the bottom. The absolute age of each layer can be dated by radiocarbon methods. Then tens of thousands of pollen grains are examined under a microscope, counted, and compared with the grains of modern pollen from known plant species.

Pollen analysis shows that Easter Island was not a wasteland at all. Instead, a subtropical forest of trees and woody bushes towered over a ground layer of shrubs, herbs, ferns, and grasses. In the forest grew tree daisies, the rope-yielding hauhau tree, a species of palm, and the toromiro tree, which furnishes a dense, mesquite-like firewood.

Pollen records show that the destruction of Easter Island's forests was well under way by the year 800, just a few centuries after the start of human settlement there. Not

A palm tree

long after 1400, palm trees became extinct and while the hauhau tree did not become extinct, its numbers declined drastically until there weren't enough left to make ropes from.

Eventually Easter Island's growing population was cutting the forest more rapidly than the forest was regrowing. The people used the land for gardens and the wood for fuel, canoes, and houses—and, of course, for transporting statues. As the forest disappeared, the islanders ran out of timber and rope to move and erect their statues. Life became more uncomfortable—springs and streams dried up, and wood was no longer available for fires.

A branch of the toromiro tree

People also found it harder to fill their stomachs as animals disappeared. Because timber for building seagoing canoes vanished, people couldn't fish. Crop yields also declined because deforestation allowed the soil to be eroded by rain and wind, dried by the sun, and its nutrients to be leeched.

With the disappearance of food sources, Easter Island could no longer feed the people who had kept a complex society running. By around 1700, the population diminished to between one-quarter and one-tenth of its former number. People started living in caves for protection against their enemies. Around 1770, rival groups started to knock down each other's statues, breaking the heads off. By 1864, the last statue had been destroyed.

Word Count: 890

Source: "Easter's End" (Diamond)

Timed Reading

Read "The Mystery of Easter Island" again. Read at a comfortable speed. Time your reading. Write your time in the Timed Reading Chart on page 235.

Start time: _____

End time: _____

My reading time: _____

After You Read

Comprehension

1. Write a statement that expresses the main idea of "The Mystery of Easter Island."

   _____

   _____

2. What can you infer in the second paragraph about the author's attitude toward Polynesian culture?

   _____

   _____

3. Write three words that describe how Easter Island looked when Roggeveen first saw it.

   _____

4. Describe in your own words the technique that scientists used to discover that Easter Island was not a wasteland in the past.

   _____

   _____

   _____

5. What was the main (or original) cause of the destruction of the Easter Island society?

   _____

   _____

Talk About It

Compare your pre- and post-reading knowledge and assumptions about Polynesian culture. What are the differences?

Before I read the passage, I . . .

I . . .

Reading 2: Cultural Ecology

Before You Read

Preview

A. The title of Reading 2 is "Cultural Ecology." The topic is the impact (effect) that human cultures have on the environment. What do you already know about how human cultures have affected the environment? What don't you know? Discuss your ideas with a partner.

B. Preview these words from the reading. Complete each sentence with the correct word.

> annihilation   immense   tangible
> decimated   reclaim   turbulent

1. There is _____, physical evidence of the Easter Island culture. The statues provide proof of the islanders' artistic abilities.

2. A(n) _____ number of species once lived there. Today, however, hundreds of animals have disappeared.

3. What led to the _____ of the Anasazi culture? For many years, scientists have investigated how the complete destruction of this lost culture happened.

4. The entire Anasazi population was _____. Some researchers think that the people killed each other.

5. The forests began to _____ their natural habitat when fires were prohibited. Other plants and animals also returned to the area.

6. There have been many _____ periods in human history. Wars and natural disasters have led to violent behavior that affected the environment.

C. These words from the reading can describe an environment. Match each with the correct definition. Write the letter of the correct answer on the line.

Words	Definitions
_____ **1.** fauna	**a.** bushes or small plants
_____ **2.** lushly	**b.** animals
_____ **3.** scrub	**c.** spread out
_____ **4.** sprawling	**d.** in a way that is full of green, healthy plants

Reading Skills

Having an Open Mind

As you learned in Chapters 1 and 2, having an open mind when you start a new reading is an important critical thinking skill. One way to have an open mind is to be aware of preconceived ideas and assumptions that you have about a topic before you read about it. Before you read, list any ideas and assumptions you have about a topic. Then, as you read, compare your ideas and assumptions with the material in the passage. Does the material confirm or disprove your assumptions? If your assumptions are incorrect, think about why you held the assumptions and how you can change them. This helps you become a better thinker, a better learner, and a better reader.

Practice

Practice becoming aware of your ideas and assumptions before and while you read. The topic of "Cultural Ecology" is the relationship between humans and their environment. With a partner, look at the title, the headings, and the pictures and captions that accompany "Cultural Ecology." Now write down all your assumptions about the topic on a separate piece of paper. Use these questions as a guide:

▶ Does the environment influence culture? How?

▶ Do cultures influence the environment? How?

▶ Did primitive cultures have less affect on the environment than modern cultures have had?

▶ Do people intentionally change or destroy the environment or does it happen accidentally?

▶ What are some ways that human cultures have affected the environment in the past?

▶ What are some tools that humans have used to affect the environment over time?

▶ Is all human interaction with the environment bad? Why or why not?

Take notes on your answers to these questions. Think about them as you read. You will compare your pre-reading answers with a partner after you read the passage.

> I am I *plus* my surroundings, and if I do not preserve the latter, I do not preserve myself. ❧
>
> — *José Ortega y Gasset (Spanish philosopher, 1883–1955)*

As You Read

As you read, think about this question:
▶ How have human cultures affected the environment?

🎧 Cultural Ecology

Evidence of the turbulent relationship between humans and their environment—from the rise and decline of empires to the annihilation of entire species—can be found throughout the world. Abandoned structures such as the toppled statues of Easter Island and barren wastelands where long-gone plants and ani-
5 mals once thrived tell the tale of the dramatic impact that humans have had on the earth. Natural environments and the resources they contain provide a framework in which human cultures can operate. Cultures, in turn, modify those environments over time. Cultural ecology is the study of this relationship between a culture group and the natural environment in which it lives. By studying cul-
10 tural ecology, we can learn how to protect the environment and ensure that cultures thrive. Let's look at human impacts on the environment in general and at human misuse of the environment.

Human Impacts

Human geography examines both the reactions of people to the physical
15 environment and the impact people have on the environment. By using our environment, we modify it—in part, through the material objects we place on the landscape: cities, farms, roads, and so on (Figure 8.1). The form these take is the product of the kind of culture group in
20 which we live. The cultural landscape, the earth's surface as modified by human action, is the tangible, physical record of a given culture. House types, transportation networks, parks, cemeteries, and the
25 size and distribution of settlements are all artifacts of the use that humans have made of the land on which they live.

Human actions, both intentional and unintentional, that modify or even

Figure 8.1: *Cape Town, South Africa, is an example of how the cultural landscape takes over the physical environment.*

destroy the environment are perhaps as old as humankind itself. People have used, altered, and replaced the vegetation over wide areas of the planet since the beginning of time. They have hunted to extinction huge groups and entire species of animals. They have, through overuse and abuse of the earth and its resources, rendered sterile and unpopulated formerly productive and attractive regions.

Fire is one of the great tools that humans have used to modify their environment, and its impact is found on nearly every continent. In many parts of the world, humans burned forests in order to allow the expansion of grasslands that supported herd animals. For example, north of the great rain forests of equatorial South America, Africa, and South Asia, lies the tropical savanna of extensive grassy vegetation separating scattered trees and forest groves (Figure 8.2). It's clear that these trees are the remains of naturally occurring tropical dry forests, thorn forests, and scrub now largely obliterated by the use, over many millennia, of fire to remove the unwanted and unproductive trees and to clear off old grasses for more nutritious new growth.

The grasses supported the immense herds of grazing animals that were the basis of hunting societies. After independence, the government of Kenya in East Africa sought to protect its national game preserves by prohibiting the periodic use of fire. Soon the immense herds of gazelles, zebras, antelope, and other grazers (and the lions and other predators that fed on them) that tourists came to see were being replaced by less appealing browsing species—rhinos, hippos, and elephants. With fire prohibited, the forests began to reclaim their natural habitat and the grassland fauna was replaced.

The same form of vegetation replacement occurred in other regions. The

Figure 8.2: *The park-like landscape of grasses and trees, characteristic of the tropical savannah found in Kenya, Africa*

grasslands of North America were greatly extended by Native Americans who burned the borders of the forest to extend grazing areas and to making hunting easier. The control of fire in modern times has resulted in the return of the forest in formerly grassy areas of Colorado, northern Arizona, and other parts of the western United States.

Human Misuse of the Environment

Examples of adverse human impact abound. The Pleistocene overkill—the Stone Age loss of whole species of large animals on all inhabited continents—is the result of the unrestricted hunting to extinction carried on by societies that used fire to trap animals and then slaughter them with axes. These two tools led to the extinction of hundreds of large mammals in Africa. In Australia, the majority of large animal, reptile, and flightless bird species had disappeared around 46,000 years ago. In North America, by 11,000 years ago, some two-thirds of original large mammals had disappeared as hunters migrated to and moved across the continent. Although some have suggested that climate changes or diseases carried by dogs, rats, and other animals were at least partially responsible, human action is the more generally accepted explanation for the abrupt changes in animal populations.

In addition, the Maoris of New Zealand and other Polynesians who had arrived in the region in the 18th century had exterminated some 80% to 90% of South Pacific bird species—as many as 2,000 in all. Similar destruction of key marine species—Caribbean sea turtles, sea cows off the coast of Australia, sea otters near Alaska, and others elsewhere—as early as 10,000 years ago, resulted in environmental damage. The effects of this damage continue to the present.

Human misuse has not only led to the destruction of animals but to the destruction of the life-supporting environment as well. For example, North Africa, the "granary of Rome" during the empire, became a wasteland due to erosion caused by inappropriate farming techniques. Easter Island in the South Pacific was covered lushly with palms and other trees when Polynesians settled there about 400 A.D. But by the beginning of the 18th century, Easter Island had become the barren wasteland it remains today. Deforestation increased soil erosion, removed the supply of trees needed to build the vital fishing canoes, and made it impossible to move the massive stone statues that were significant in the islanders' religion (Figure 8.3). With the loss of livelihood resources and the collapse of religion, warfare broke out and the population was decimated. A similar tragic sequence is occurring on Madagascar in the Indian Ocean today. Despite romantic notions about the close connection between the early societies and the environment, not all early societies lived in harmony with the environment.

95 The more technologically advanced and complex the culture, the more apparent is its impact on the natural landscape. In sprawling urban-industrial societies, the cultural landscape—

100 buildings, roads, cell phone towers—outweighs the natural physical environment in its impact on people's daily lives. It interposes itself between "nature" and

Figure 8.3: *Stone statue on Easter Island*

105 humans, and residents of the cities of such societies—living and working in climate-controlled buildings, driving to enclosed shopping malls—can go through life having very little contact with or concern about the physical environment.

Word Count: 1,051

Source: *Human Geography* (Fellmann, Getis, Getis, and Malinowski)

Timed Reading

Read "Cultural Ecology" again. Read at a comfortable speed. Time your reading. Write your time in the Timed Reading Chart on page 235.

Start time: _____

End time: _____

My reading time: _____

After You Read

Main Idea

Look at the ideas and assumptions you wrote before reading "Cultural Ecology." Which were correct? Which were incorrect?

_____

_____

Reading Skills

Identifying Causes and Effects

When you read about human geography, it's important to understand the causes and effects of events. Some effects are the immediate result of a cause. Sometimes, there is a chain of causes that result in a certain effect.

One way to understand causes and effects is to use a graphic organizer. Look at this example of a causal chain graphic organizer. It illustrates an aspect of global warming and answers the question: How can deforestation cause other life forms to disappear?

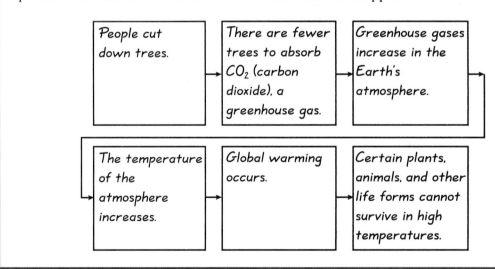

Practice

How did the impact of humans on their environment lead to the disappearance of the Easter Island society? Use the causal chain graphic organizer on the next page to show how this happened.

Put these events in the correct order in the chart:

▶ The soil lost its nutrients.
▶ There wasn't enough food; the population diminished.

▶ Easter Islanders cut down too many trees.
▶ Crops couldn't grow.
▶ The island became deforested.

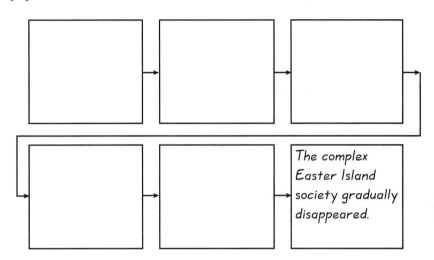

The complex Easter Island society gradually disappeared.

Getting the Details

Answer these questions about "Cultural Ecology." If the question refers to causes or effects, draw graphic organizers on a separate piece of paper.

1. What are some of the tangible results of human modification of the Earth's surface?

_____

_____

2. How has the use of fire affected the animal populations in some parts of the world?

_____

_____

3. Why did Native Americans burn the borders of forests? _____

_____

4. What was the result of the "Pleistocene overkill"? _____

_____

5. Why is North Africa a wasteland?_____

_____

Vocabulary

A. Here are some more words and expressions from "Cultural Ecology." Find them in the reading and circle them.

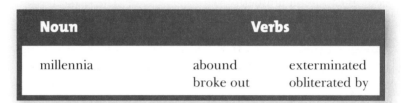

Noun	Verbs	
millennia	abound	exterminated
	broke out	obliterated by

B. Now use them to complete the sentences.

1. The Maoris _____ many bird species. In fact, they destroyed about 2,000 different ones.

2. Warfare _____ after resources began disappearing on Easter Island. The breakdown of the culture caused many conflicts.

3. Humans have used fire to modify their environment over many _____. It has been an important human tool for thousands of years.

4. Examples of disappearing species _____. There are many examples of endangered species all over the world.

5. Very few trees remain in the tropical savanna. They were _____ the use of fire thousands of years ago.

Talk About It

Discuss these questions.

1. What can individuals do to improve the environment? What can groups do? What should governments do?
2. Are you optimistic about the future of the environment? Why or why not?

Expressions

> ## Collocations for Discussing Human Impact on the Environment
>
> Collocations are words that are frequently used together. Here are some collocations from "The Mystery of Easter Island" and "Cultural Ecology." They relate to human impact on the environment. Try to memorize them.
>
> | | |
> |---|---|
> | (be) carried on by | hunted to extinction |
> | clear off | knock (something) down |
> | the cultural landscape | migrated to |
> | dried up | ran out of |
>
> When you learn collocations, notice how they are used in a sentence. Notice also the entire expression. For example, notice both the verb and the preposition(s).
>
> **Examples:**
>
> Deforestation **was carried on by** many societies. For example, both the Anasazi and the Easter Islanders practiced it.
>
> Many cultures used fire to **clear off** old plants. The removal of old growth allowed new plants to grow.

Practice

A. Find and underline the collocations in the box above in "The Mystery of Easter Island" and "Cultural Ecology."

B. Now use some of them to complete the sentences.

1. When the Easter Islanders _____ wood, they didn't have enough fuel to keep warm or cook food.

2. Did the islanders _____ the statues _____? No one knows, but many of them are no longer standing.

3. _____ refers to the surface of the earth as modified by human actions.

4. When the springs and streams _____, there wasn't enough water for people to drink.

5. Hunters left where they were and _____ other parts of the continent. As they moved across the land, they killed many large mammals.

Internet Research

Identifying Unbiased Information on the Internet

When you do Internet research, it's important to know if the information you find is unbiased (fair, neutral). This is especially true if you are doing scientific research. Here are some ways to help you to determine if the information on a website is unbiased:

1. Look for information about the organization that is responsible for the website. To do this, look for a mission statement, a *Welcome* statement, or an *About Us* link.

2. As you read about the organization or institution responsible for the website, try to find out:
   ▶ where they get their information
   ▶ how they get their information
   ▶ who the information is for
   ▶ what kind of information it is; that is, is it opinion or scientific research? Does the organization have a position on an issue, or are they neutral?

Note: Any website, regardless of the URL (.edu, .gov, .com, or .org), can have biased information. Therefore, you should always use your critical thinking skills when you read websites.

Practice

Do an Internet search for information on a lost civilization. First, evaluate your search results by looking at the URLs. Then go to websites that look unbiased and try to determine if the information on the website is in fact unbiased. Choose the best website(s) and take notes on the information to use later. Finally, tell the class about your results.

Write About It

Write paragraphs about human cultures and the environment. Choose one of these topics:

▶ Explain what you are doing to preserve the environment.
▶ What lost civilization interests you? Explain why it interests you. How did it disappear?

Use five words and expressions from this chapter. Also, try to use your Internet research.

On Your Own

Project

Give a presentation on a "lost" civilization.

Step 1: Prepare

Choose a civilization. It can be the one you researched for the Internet activity on page 182 or another. Find out about the civilization and the people: Where and how did they live? What kind of resources did they have? Have any artifacts of their civilization survived to this day? What were the causes of their disappearance?

Write notes for your presentation in the box below or on a separate piece of paper. If you can, bring in pictures and use captions with the pictures. Practice your presentation with a partner.

Civilization and location: _____

Lifestyle: _____

Resources: _____

Examples (if any) of artifacts that have survived: _____

_____

_____

_____

Causes of their disappearance: _____

_____

_____

Step 2: Give the Presentation

Give your presentation in small groups. Take turns speaking. Make eye contact with (look into the eyes of) your audience. The audience should take notes and ask questions.

Step 3: Follow-Up

Discuss your presentations. Which were interesting? What made them interesting? What will you do differently the next time that you give a presentation?

How Much Do You Remember?

Check your new knowledge. In this chapter you learned facts, words, and expressions. You also learned reading skills and you practiced writing. Complete the following to check what you remember.

1. What are two tools humans have used for millennia to change the environment? _____

   _____

   _____

2. What is the purpose of having an open mind when you approach new material? _____

   _____

   _____

3. Use *annihilation* in a sentence. _____

   _____

4. Use *hunted to extinction* in a sentence. _____

   _____

5. Explain how another civilization (in addition to Easter Island) disappeared. _____

   _____

   _____

6. What kind of information should you look for in a website when you are doing research on a

   scientific topic? _____

   _____

Second Timed Readings

Now reread "The Mystery of Easter Island" and "Cultural Ecology." Time each reading separately. Write your times in the Timed Reading Chart on page 235.

Crossword Puzzle

Complete the crossword puzzle to practice some words and expressions from this chapter.

CLUES

Across →
1. The act of removing trees
5. Spread out
9. Without life
10. Many birds in Polynesia were hunted to _____.
12. A place where nothing grows

Down ↓
2. Killed
3. Moved to
4. Thousands of years
6. Very large

7. When the rivers did this, there wasn't enough water for the Easter Islanders.
8. Easter Islanders began to _____ the statues.
11. Violent

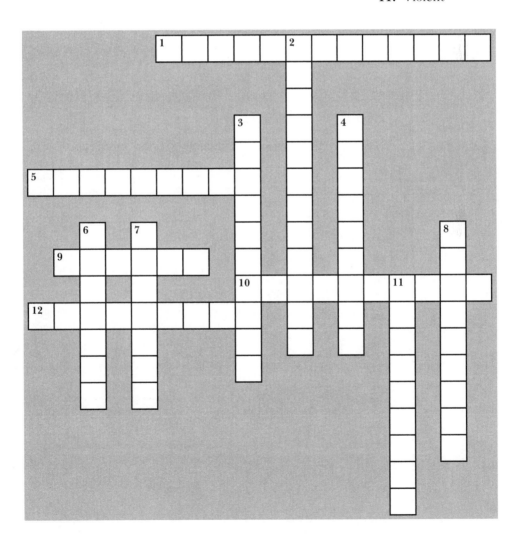

UNIT 5 Biology

What is Biology?

Biology is the study of living things and their environments. Biologists study plants, animals, and humans. Biologists also improve food crops, develop medicines, and work with animals and their habitats. Other areas in biology include:

- plant biology
- animal behavior
- ecology
- genetics
- biochemistry
- cell biology
- microbiology

Biology began with prehistoric people, who knew the difference between poisonous and nonpoisonous plants. The ancient Egyptians, Babylonians, and Greeks left records of their work in biology. For example, the Greek philosopher Aristotle (384–322 B.C.) studied medicine, and classified and described many life forms.

SOME FAMOUS BIOLOGISTS

Anton van Leeuwenhoek—Dutch, 1632–1723

Carl Linnaeus—Swedish, 1707–1778

Charles Darwin—English, 1809–1882

Gregor Mendel—Austrian, 1822–1884

Barbara McClintock—American, 1902–1992

Francis Harry Compton Crick—English, 1916–2004

Biology and You

Biologists work with animals in zoos or botanical gardens. Some do research for government agencies, pharmaceutical companies, or hospitals. Biologists also write for technical publications.

Do you want to study biology? Ask yourself these questions:

- Am I interested in plants, animals, and people?
- Do I like science?
- Am I good at observing and describing?
- Do I enjoy doing experiments?
- Am I careful and patient?
- Am I a creative thinker?

CHAPTER 9 Cloning

CHAPTER PREVIEW

In this chapter, you'll:

Content
▶ learn about a cloned cat
▶ read about the ethics of cloning

Reading Skills
▶ combine skills to preview a reading
▶ form opinions

Vocabulary Skills
▶ use words and expressions for discussing cloning and the ethics of cloning
▶ use collocations to discuss cloning

Writing Skills
▶ express your opinion about cloning

Internet Skills
▶ use the Internet to find the latest news about cloning

> Cloning may be good and it may be bad. Probably it's a bit of both. 🐑
>
> —*Richard Dawkins (British evolutionary biologist, b. 1941)*

SHORT SURVEY

In my opinion . . .

❑ cloning* is O.K. for medical purposes only.

❑ cloning is only O.K. for agricultural purposes—so people in developing countries can have more food.

❑ cloning should not be done under any circumstances.

❑ there should be no restrictions on cloning.

❑ other: _____

*copying cells or DNA

Reading 1:

Would a clone of your pet cat be an exact copy? Read about a company that clones pets to find out.

Reading 2:

What are the ethical issues surrounding cloning? Find out in "The Ethics of Cloning."

What do you think?

Read the questions in the box. Choose one or more to discuss with a partner. Give reasons for your opinions.

1. Should animals be used in scientific experiments? Why or why not?

2. Should people's medical records be private? Why or why not?

3. Should private companies own the rights to the genetic information of animals or plants? Why or why not?

4. Who should have the right to see and use an individual's genes and genetic information? Why?

5. Is genetically modified food safe? Should it be given to people in developing countries? Why or why not?

6. Should governments spend large amounts of money on scientific research that has no direct benefit for humans? Why or why not?

7. Should governments regulate scientific research? Why or why not?

8. Should drugs that are essential for keeping people healthy or alive (such as AIDS medications) be free? Why or why not?

9. Should genetic engineering be used to improve humans (e.g., in terms of athletic performance, intelligence, or appearance)? Why or why not?

10. Should anyone be able to have children by *in vitro* fertilization (fertilization in a laboratory instead of in a human body)? Why or why not?

11. Should people be allowed to clone their pets? Why or why not?

12. Should the cloning of humans be allowed? Why or why not?

> We thought this wasn't possible and that we didn't have to worry about it for a while. Then it happened. ❧
>
> —Dianne Bartels (American biomedical ethicist b. 1943)

Reading 1: Cloned Cat is No Copycat

Before You Read

Preview

A. Reading 1 is a newspaper article entitled "Cloned Cat is No Copycat." A *copycat* is a person or thing that imitates (does the same things as) another person or thing. Based on this information, what do you think the article will be about? Discuss your ideas with a partner.

B. Preview some of the main ideas in the reading by taking the following True/False quiz. Circle *T* (True) or *F* (False).

1. A cloned cat will look the same as the cat it was cloned from.	T	F
2. A cloned cat will behave the same as the cat it was cloned from.	T	F
3. A cloned cat will have the same personality as the cat it was cloned from.	T	F
4. Barnyard animals such as goats and cows have not been successfully cloned.	T	F
5. Dogs have not been successfully cloned.	T	F
6. Animal lovers tend to bond with (become close to) their pets because of the pet's personality.	T	F

> Cloning is not photocopying. 🐾
>
> — *Peter Cochrane*
> *(British futurist, b. 1946)*

Vocabulary

Here are some words and expressions from "Cloned Cat is No Copycat." Match them with the highlighted words or expressions in the sentences. Write the letter of the correct answer on the line.

> a. a déluge
> b. espoused
> c. euthanized
> d. exploit
> e. has been neutered
> f. misperception
> g. resurrect
> h. sparked
> i. vindicates

_____ **1.** The company that successfully cloned a cat received **a large number** of requests from people who wanted to duplicate their pets.

_____ **2.** The cloned animal was too sick to survive, so the researchers had it **killed in a humane way**.

_____ **3.** Skippy, Jane's dog, **has had a procedure that makes him unable to reproduce**.

_____ **4.** Some people think that cloning is a way to **bring back to life** a beloved pet.

_____ **5.** The company's experiments with cloning **caused** a great deal of interest in duplicating pets.

_____ **6.** It is unethical to **take advantage of** people's confusion about the reality of cloning.

_____ **7.** The **misunderstanding** that many people have about cloning is that it creates an exact duplicate.

_____ **8.** The result of the cloning experiment **justifies** what the experts have been saying for a long time.

_____ **9.** For a long time, experts **strongly believed and promoted** the idea that cloning does not lead to duplication.

As You Read

As you read, think about this question:
▶ In what ways will a cloned animal be like the original, and in what ways will it be different?

🎧 Cloned Cat is No Copycat

Rainbow the cat is a typical calico with splotches of brown, tan, and gold on white. Cc (for "carbon copy"), her clone, has a striped gray coat over white. Rainbow is reserved. Cc is curious and playful. Rainbow is chunky. Cc is sleek. Wayne Pacelle of the Humane Society might be inclined to say: I told you so. But then, so would Cc's creators at Texas A&M University. Sure, you can clone your favorite cat. But the copy will not necessarily act or even look like the original.

Cc was born on Dec. 22, 2001. Her birth was big news when it was announced because it was the first time a household pet had been cloned. Previous mammal clones were barnyard animals like cows and goats.

Rainbow and her clone Cc

Cc's creation was funded by Genetic Savings & Clone, a company that hopes to make money from people's desires to duplicate their favorite pets. "But people who hope cloning will resurrect a pet will be disappointed," said Duane Kraemer, one of A&M's animal cloning experts.

Experts say environment is as important as genes in determining a cat's personality. And as far as appearance goes, having the same DNA as another calico cat doesn't always produce the same coat pattern.

"This vindicates the opposition we espoused from the beginning, that cloning does not lead to duplication," said Pacelle, senior vice president of the Humane Society of the United States.

"Not only does cloning not produce a physical duplicate, but it can never reproduce the behavior or personality of a cat that you want to keep around. There are millions of cats in shelters and with rescue groups that need homes, and the last thing we need is to produce more cats."

Hundreds of Samples

Before the birth of Cc, Genetic Savings & Clone had hundreds of pet DNA samples stored at a cost of $895 for healthy animals and $1,395 for sick or dead animals.

Lou Hawthorne, Genetic Savings & Clone chief executive, estimated that the cost to create a clone will initially be in the low five figures and later drop to the low four figures.

"Though Cc's arrival sparked a déluge of calls from pet owners, more research is needed to figure out how to produce consistently healthy clones before the company can start doing it commercially," said Ben Carlson, the company's spokesman.

"A year ago, we said we'd start commercial services in a year, and here we are a year later,"

Carlson said. "It's really impossible for us to make a certain prediction as to how long it's going to take to develop the technology to get successful results."

There is a demand from dog lovers, but scientists so far have been unable to clone a dog.

In fact, Cc's creation was the result of a dog lover, not a cat lover. University of Phoenix founder John Sperling wanted a duplicate of his collie mix, Missy. With his $3.7 million, Texas A&M launched the "Missyplicity" project over four years ago.

Now, Missy is dead, euthanized last year because of an inoperable growth in her throat. Sperling has redirected his funding to the Sausalito, California-based Genetic Savings & Clone, which he hopes will one day deliver a clone of Missy.

Turning Away Customers

Carlson said the company tells pet owners that cloning won't resurrect their pet and that the company has turned away some customers clearly interested in getting the same animal.

"In the short term, it's easy to exploit that misperception," he said. "But in the long term, it's unethical, and the pet owner will quickly find that, 'Hey, this isn't Fluffy. This puppy doesn't recognize me or know all the old tricks.'"

However, he said cloning could reproduce what a pet owner considers to be exceptional genes, particularly from an animal with unknown parentage or one that has been spayed or neutered.

"A small percentage of the population knows exactly what they want and they want to stick with it—another animal as similar as possible," Carlson said. "That's the motive we've encountered among our clients."

"But disclaimers could go unheard by pet owners desperate to duplicate an animal," said University of Pennsylvania bioethicist Arthur Caplan, a critic of pet cloning and companies that purport to sell it.

He said animal lovers bond with pets because of their personalities and behaviors, not the genetic material.

"The new cloned dog won't know the old tricks—you have to teach them," Caplan said. "It doesn't matter how many genes they have in common."

Word Count: 763

Source: "A Year Later, Cloned Cat is No Copycat" (Hays)

Timed Reading

Read "Cloned Cat is No Copycat" again. Read at a comfortable speed. Time your reading. Write your time in the Timed Reading Chart on page 236.

Start time: _____

End time: _____

My reading time: _____

After You Read

Comprehension

1. In what way is Cc like Rainbow? In what way is she different? _____

_____

2. Why was Cc's birth "big news"? _____

_____

3. Describe the differences between Rainbow and Cc. _____

_____

4. Why does Duane Kraemer, one of A&M's animal cloning experts, say that people who hope that cloning will resurrect a pet will be disappointed?

_____

_____

5. According to the article, what do many people seem to believe about cloning?

_____

_____

6. Review your answers to the True/False quiz on page 190. For any incorrect answers, write the true statement on the lines below.

_____

_____

_____

Talk About It

Discuss these questions.

1. Were you surprised by any of the information in Reading 1? Explain your answer.

2. Do you have a pet? Would you be interested in cloning it? Why or why not?

Reading 2: The Ethics of Cloning

Before You Read

Reading Skills

> ### Putting It All Together to Preview
>
> In previous chapters, you used titles, headings, pictures and captions, introductions and conclusions, and topic sentences to preview a reading. Together, these strategies are powerful previewing tools. You can combine all or some of these skills. Practice combining previewing skills whenever you start a new reading.

Practice

Answer the following questions to practice combining previewing skills.

1. What is the title of Reading 2 (page 198)? _____

   What do you think it will be about? _____

   _____

   _____

2. Read the introduction. What background information is in the introduction?

   _____

   _____

   _____

3. Read the four headings in the passage and write what you think each section might be about.

   Section 1: _____

   _____

   _____

   Section 2: _____

   _____

   _____

Section 3: _____

_____

_____

Section 4: _____

_____

_____

4. Read and underline the first sentence of Paragraphs 2, 3, and 6. Then write what you think the paragraph is about.

Paragraph 2: _____

_____

_____

Paragraph 3: _____

_____

_____

Paragraph 6: _____

_____

_____

5. Look at the pictures and read the captions. Why do you think these pictures are here? What do

they tell you? _____

_____

_____

_____

Preview

A. The title of Reading 2 is "The Ethics of Cloning." Based on the preview practice you already did, what do you think the reading is about? Discuss your ideas with a partner.

B. Preview these words and expressions from the reading. Match each word or expression with the correct definition. Write the letter of the correct answer on the line.

Words	Definitions
_____ **1.** defense	**a.** human DNA
_____ **2.** embryos	**b.** relating to
_____ **3.** human genome	**c.** serious
_____ **4.** infertile	**d.** variety; differences
_____ **5.** profound	**e.** protection
_____ **6.** resistance	**f.** belief; theory; idea
_____ **7.** sequenced	**g.** not able to have children
_____ **8.** supposition	**h.** fighting off the effects of something
_____ **9.** surrounding	**i.** ordered; shown in order
_____ **10.** variation	**j.** the early stage of development of living organisms before birth

DNA

As you read, think about these questions:

▶ What aspect of cloning is the most controversial? Why?

> The fuss about cloning is rather silly. I can't see any essential distinction between cloning and producing brothers and sisters in the time-honored way. 🐑
>
> — *Stephen Hawking (British astrophysicist, b. 1942)*

🎧 The Ethics of Cloning

Few scientific advances have created a media uproar like that seen over Dolly—the lamb cloned in Scotland from an adult sheep. While the advance is of undoubted scientific importance and may aid agriculture and medicine substantially, the same might be said of any number of other scientific advances in recent years. What is it about Dolly that creates such fear and

5 unrest among the general public?

Human Cloning

The fear of human cloning is of course at the heart of the public's discomfort. While cloning procedures are still inefficient, there seems to be no technical reason why it would not be possible to clone a

10 human. Indeed, Italian scientists announced in 2001 that they were proceeding to do just that. Their plan to clone children for infertile couples was met with a storm of protest. Because cloning procedures are so inefficient, most embryos in such a procedure would not be expected to survive. Is it ethical to form so many human embryos con-

15 demned to die in order to make sure that one will live? The prospect of cloning humans raises many issues such as these.

Dolly the sheep, the world's first cloned mammal, born in 1996

Cloning and Individuality

Even if the technology is perfected, the cloning of humans raises profound issues of personal identity. If you were to clone a child, the initial cell of the clone, the cell that would go on to form

20 a child in your image, would be in every way the same as the cell that made YOU. What is there to worry about in this? What is so wrong about this cell that was so right about you?

An obvious answer is that we look for individuality in every person. Deeply ingrained in many cultures is the supposition that people are all different from one another, and that these differences are an essential part of the human condition. For example, when the American statesman Thomas Jefferson wrote that "We hold these truths to be self-evident, that all men are created equal . . . ," he didn't mean that people are all clones, genetically equal to one another, but rather that, despite all our differences, every person ought to be equal under the law. Why treat every person equally? Because, when we were conceived, the genetic dice were rolled for all of us equally. How we turn out as people, Jefferson believed, depended largely on opportunity, which should be the same for all. This sense of individual self-worth lies at the heart of democracy, and is an integral part of the laws of many nations.

Careful studies of identical twins over the last decade have produced very strong evidence that much of the variation in personality and intelligence between humans is inherited. Only some 30% of the variation among individuals in these traits reflects differences in experience, in how they were raised and educated. A bunch of clones would differ from one another by just that much. Is 30% of the variation among us enough to sustain our view of individual uniqueness?

The Urge to "Better" Humankind

One of the strongest of the ethical issues surrounding human cloning is the temptation to yield to the understandable urge to "better" humankind, to achieve in the short run what evolution strives for in the long run. The danger, of course, lies in assuming that we know what will happen in the long run.

Identical twins

But the temptation may be difficult to resist. With the human genome sequenced, it will not be long before the genes responsible for most hereditary disorders are identified. Advances in gene therapy are increasingly allowing the transfer of healthy genes to replace defective ones. As cloning technology is perfected, it becomes possible to contemplate creating a child by cloning one of the parents, in the process "correcting" any gene defects. For example, it may be possible to eliminate in the cloned "child" the gene for breast cancer that the mother carries. A perfect child is the hope of every parent. It is difficult to imagine a more cloudy ethical issue.

Genetic Uniformity and Disease

An even more profound problem arises from another direction, one that many people are unaware of: because cloning promotes genetic uniformity, making our genes more like each other's, cloning increases the danger that at some future time a disease might arise against which the "common" cloned form has no resistance. Genetic variation is the chief defense our species has against an uncertain future. To strip ourselves of it, even partially, is to endanger 60 our species.

Asexual reproduction, in which all offspring are genetically identical clones, is common in nature in both plants (dandelions are a common example) and animals (some lizard species have only females), but usually only in extreme or high-risk environments, where survival is uncertain. Nature has not favored asexual reproduction in any mammal because the 30% of 65 variation due to nurture is just not enough protection against an uncertain future if you are going to make a major investment in each offspring. It is, thus, the very nature of our species that places such value on variation among individuals, perhaps the deepest and most compelling reason to carefully consider the implications of human cloning before proceeding.

Word Count: 963

Source: *The Living World* (Johnson)

Timed Reading

Read "The Ethics of Cloning" again. Read at a comfortable speed. Time your reading. Write your time in the Timed Reading Chart on page 236.

Start time: _____

End time: _____

My reading time: _____

After You Read

Main Idea

Write a statement that expresses the main issues surrounding the cloning of humans.

_____

_____

_____

Getting the Details

Answer the following questions. Use complete sentences.

1. According to the author, what leads to individuality in humans?

_____

_____

_____

2. What have twin studies shown about personality and intelligence?

_____

_____

_____

3. What is one example of the *urge to "better" humankind*?

_____

4. According to the author, would many parents be tempted to have a genetically "perfect" child? Explain.

_____

5. Explain in your own words the possible health problems that genetically identical clones might face. _____

_____

_____

6. What is "perhaps the deepest and most compelling reason to carefully consider the implications of human cloning before proceeding," according to the author? _____

_____

_____

_____

Reading Skills

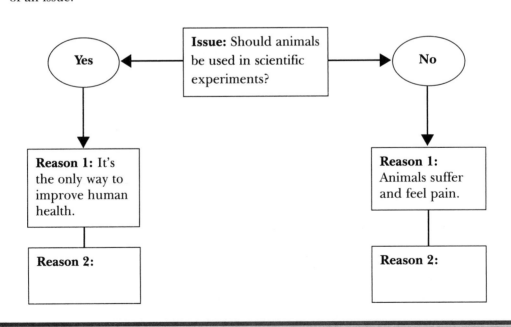

Forming an Opinion

Ethical questions often have two or more perspectives or sides. Critical thinkers are able to see all of the sides of an issue. At the same time, they can take either side of an issue and support it.

One way to do this is to look at all aspects of an issue and consider the ideas that support each one. By doing this, you can often choose the most logical side.

Here's an example of a simple graphic organizer that can help you look at two sides of an issue:

Issue: Should animals be used in scientific experiments?

Yes

No

Reason 1: It's the only way to improve human health.

Reason 2:

Reason 1: Animals suffer and feel pain.

Reason 2:

Practice

Choose one of the ethical issues on page 189 and write it in the Issue box below. Use the graphic organizer to show the sides of the issue. Try to write at least three reasons for each side. Then choose the side that makes the most sense to you. Write a statement that expresses your opinion and the reasons for it.

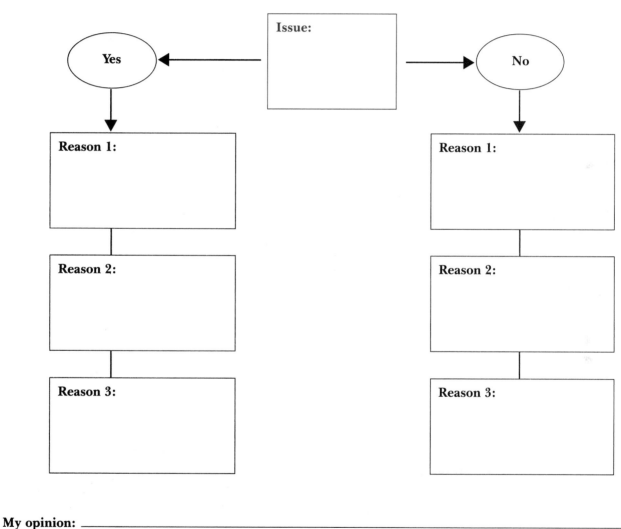

Issue:

Yes

No

Reason 1:

Reason 2:

Reason 3:

Reason 1:

Reason 2:

Reason 3:

My opinion: _____

_____

_____

_____

Vocabulary

A. Here are some more words and expressions from "The Ethics of Cloning." Find them in the reading and circle them.

Verbs	Adjective	Expressions
a. strip ourselves of b. turn out as	c. cloudy	d. at the heart of f. the (genetic) dice were rolled for all of us

B. Now match each word in the box with the highlighted words or expressions in the sentences. Write the letter of the correct answer on the line.

_____ **1.** Twin studies have shown that how we **become** individuals depends on our environment.

_____ **2.** When we were conceived, **we had the same chances as anyone else**.

_____ **3.** The desire for a perfect child raises some ethical issues that are **not clear**.

_____ **4.** Human identity is **the central issue in** the debate about cloning.

_____ **5.** If we **remove** genetic variation, we may not be able to survive.

Talk About It

Discuss these questions.

1. What was your opinion about cloning before you read "The Ethics of Cloning"? Has it changed? Why or why not?
2. Is it necessary to restrict cloning completely in order to avoid misuses of the technology? Why or why not?
3. Should cloning be controlled? If yes, who should control it (e.g., the government, private organizations, or individuals)?

Expressions

Collocations for Discussing Cloning

Collocations are words that are frequently used together. Here are some useful collocations for discussing cloning:

creates fear	**in the long run/term**
gene therapy	**in the short run/term**
to get successful results	**raises (profound) issues**
hereditary disorders	**scientific advances**

Examples:

Even if cloning can eliminate **hereditary disorders**, many people are against the artificial improvement of humans.

Cloning perfects organisms **in the short run**, while evolution makes improvements over a longer period of time.

Practice

A. Find and underline the collocations in the box above in "Cloned Cat is No Copycat" and "The Ethics of Cloning."

B. Now use some of them to complete the sentences.

1. _____ in the areas of cloning and robotics force people to consider what it means to be human.

2. _____ is (are) replacing faulty genes with healthy, artificial copies.

3. For many years, people thought that cloning wasn't possible. Now that it's happened, it

   _____ about what it means to be human.

4. Cloning technology is developed enough _____. Many cloned animals are healthy and live long lives.

5. Cloning _____ in many people because they don't really understand it.

6. Genetic Savings & Clone has been successful so far, but will the company survive

   _____?

Internet Research

Finding News on the Internet

You can find recent news stories on topics such as cloning in online newspapers and magazines. Most publications have websites that provide free access to recent news stories. You may have to register on the website (which is usually free), and you may have to pay for news that is over a week old. To find a news story, use the *Search* function to do a keyword search for recent news. If you search in the *Archives* (a collection of older stories), you may have to pay to read the entire story. Note that the date and the name of the newspaper will appear in the results. This can help you choose the best articles.

Some websites such as Google (**www.google.com**) and Yahoo (**www.yahoo.com**) also have current news. To get news, look for the *News* section, and click on it. When you get to the news area, type the topic that you want into the search box.

Practice

Look at an online newspaper, magazine, or website such as Google or Yahoo for recent news about cloning: the cloning of pets, human cloning, the ethics of cloning, twin studies, or another aspect of cloning that interests you. Print the best news story and bring it to class.

With a partner discuss the following questions:

▶ What keywords did you use?

▶ Which newspapers had the best (most interesting, closest to the topic, most factual, most recent) results?

▶ On what date were the stories published?

Write About It

Write about your opinion on one of the following topics:

▶ the cloning of humans

▶ the cloning of pets

▶ one of the ethical questions on page 189

Give at least three reasons for your opinion. Use five words and expressions from this chapter. Also, try to use your Internet research.

On Your Own

Project

Debate cloning or one of the ethical questions on page 189.

Step 1: Prepare

Get into groups of six. Choose an issue. Have three group members take the pro side—the side that agrees with the issue—and the other three take the con side—the side that disagrees with the issue. (You don't have to take the side that you actually believe in.)

Work separately with your team to select three reasons for your side of the issue. Also, try to predict the reasons the other side will have. Make notes on your reasons. Use a graphic organizer or the box below.

Issue:	
Pro Side:_____	Con Side:_____
_____	_____
Reason 1:_____	Reason 1:_____
_____	_____
Reason 2:_____	Reason 2:_____
_____	_____
Reason 3:_____	Reason 3:_____
_____	_____

Step 2: Give the Debate

Give your debate for the class. Each person can present one reason. As you listen to each group's debate, focus on the reasons each team presents and decide which team in each group has the strongest arguments.

Step 3: Follow-Up

Discuss your debates. Which topics were the most interesting? Why or why not? Which teams gave the most convincing reasons? Did any of the teams' reasons influence you? Why or why not?

Wrap Up

How Much Do You Remember?

Check your new knowledge. In this chapter you learned facts, words, and expressions. You also learned reading skills and you practiced writing. Complete the following to check what you remember.

1. How is a cloned cat likely to be different from the original? _____

   _____

2. What aspect of humanity does cloning threaten, according to "The Ethics of Cloning"? _____

   _____

3. Use *resistant* in a sentence. _____

   _____

   _____

4. What is one way to develop an informed opinion about a controversial issue? _____

   _____

   _____

5. Use *gene therapy* in a sentence. _____

   _____

6. Use *in the long run* in a sentence. _____

   _____

7. What are two ways to find recent news on the Internet? _____

   _____

   _____

Second Timed Readings

Now reread "Cloned Cat is No Copycat" and "The Ethics of Cloning." Time each reading separately. Write your times in the Timed Reading Chart on page 236.

Crossword Puzzle

Complete the crossword puzzle to practice some words and expressions from this chapter.

CLUES

Across →
1. Bring back to life
6. It may be dangerous to ___ ourselves of our genetic variation.
7. Killed in a humane way
8. Copying cells or DNA
9. Unable to have children

Down ↓
2. Theory
3. The ability to avoid something
4. Differences
5. Unclear

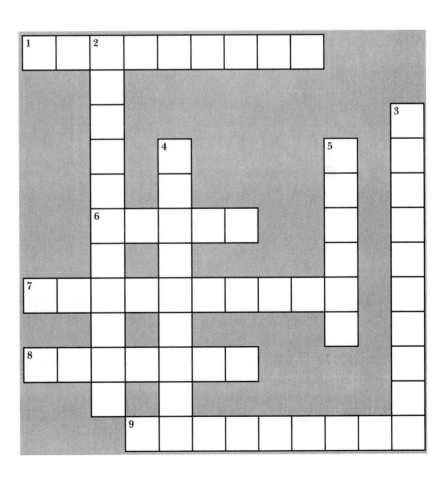

CHAPTER 10 Animal Communication

CHAPTER PREVIEW

In this chapter, you'll:

Content
▶ find out secrets of cross-species communication
▶ learn how animals signal danger

Reading Skills
▶ preview by using your own approach
▶ use notes to write a summary

Vocabulary Skills
▶ use words and expressions used to talk about animal communication
▶ use collocations to discuss animal communication

Writing Skills
▶ write about animal and human communication

Internet Skills
▶ find specific information on a webpage

> If you talk to the animals, they will talk with you and you will know each other. If you do not talk to them, you will not know them, and what you do not know you will fear. What one fears one destroys. 🌿
>
> — *Chief Dan George (Chief of Salish Band in Burrard Inlet, British Columbia and actor, 1899–1982)*

SHORT SURVEY

I think animals communicate (check all that apply):

❑ easily with humans

❑ differently from humans

❑ to attract a mate

❑ to repel an enemy

❑ to send information about a food source

❑ other: _____

Reading 1:
What works when training an animal? "Secrets of Cross-species Communication" has some answers.

Reading 2:
How do animals communicate danger to one another? Find out in "How Animals Signal Danger."

What do you think?

Answer the questions about animals and communication. Also, write an explanation for each answer. Guess if you're not sure. Then ask your partner the questions. Write your partner's answers in the box. Compare and discuss your answers.

Animal Communication		
Questions	**My Answers**	**My Partner's Answers**
1. What pets do you, your family, or your friends have?		
2. Do most people find it easy or hard to train animals?		
3. Do most people communicate easily with animals such as dogs, horses, or camels?		
4. Do animal trainers all over the world use the same sounds to make animals go faster?		
5. Do animals use sounds to signal danger?		
6. Do animals of the same species use similar sounds for romance?		
7. Do animals of the same species use similar sounds for danger?		
8. Do monkeys use the same calls for all kinds of danger?		
9. Do animals use danger calls only to ask for help? If not, for what other reasons might they use danger calls?		

Reading 1: Secrets of Cross-species Communication

Before You Read

Preview

A. The title of Reading 1 is "Secrets of Cross-species Communication." What do you think "cross-species" means? What do you think you will learn in this reading? Discuss your ideas with a partner.

B. In "Secrets of Cross-species Communication," the author discusses physical communication and auditory (sound) communication with animals. Discuss your opinions about the connection between physical communication and auditory communication with animals. Read each situation below and discuss if you agree or disagree. Make sure you explain your opinion.

Physical Communication with Animals

1. If a dog jumps up to lick your hand, the best thing to do is push the dog down.

2. If a dog sees people's legs streched out in front of them, it "reads" anger.

3. Dogs hit or block other dogs to show that they want more space.

Auditory Communication with Animals

1. Some dogs can be trained to walk toward sheep, circle around them, and then lie down when they hear whistle commands.

2. In training dogs, it's important to use sounds that are easy to distinguish.

3. All animal trainers use the same kinds of sounds to call animals.

Talk About It

Discuss these questions.
Is communicating with animals important? Why or why not? For example, can learning to communicate with one species help you communicate with other species? Explain your answer.

Is communicating with animals important?

I . . .

Vocabulary

Here are some words from "Secrets of Cross-species Communication." Match each word with the correct definition below. Write the letter of the correct answer on the line.

a. behavioral	d. handlers	g. syndicated	j. whoa
b. epiphany	e. hips	h. vital	
c. frequency	f. soothe	i. wags	

_____ **1.** the joints below the waist and above the thigh that allow the legs to move

_____ **2.** moves back and forth

_____ **3.** relating to a way of acting or reacting

_____ **4.** critical; important

_____ **5.** make calm; quiet

_____ **6.** sound made to stop horses from moving

_____ **7.** appearing on many radio or TV stations

_____ **8.** people who train, direct, or control animals

_____ **9.** the number of cycles per second of a sound determining the pitch

_____ **10.** sudden insight or awareness

> An animal's eyes have the power to speak a great language. ❧
>
> —*Martin Buber (Jewish philosopher, 1878–1965)*

As you read, think about this question:

▶ What is one secret of cross-species communication?

🎧 Secrets of Cross-species Communication

Dr. Patricia McConnell with lamb and Border collie

Upon a stage in front of a packed auditorium, Patricia McConnell conducts a simple demonstration. Before her is a wiggling young dog who periodically jumps up to try and lick her hands.

5 First, Patricia shows the audience an ineffective way to teach a dog not to jump: she reaches toward the jumping dog with her hand to push it down. It's natural for primates to push, and it's a signal we readily understand. However, to a dog, outstretched

10 front legs are an invitation to play. That's the message this dog is getting, and it wags its tail even harder and jumps again.

Next, Patricia demonstrates how to make this cross-species communication more effective. Dogs that want some personal space use a shoulder slam or body block to get it. This time when the dog jumps, Patricia swings her hips

15 into it, keeping her hands at her side. The dog quickly gets the message, and soon sits back on its haunches when Patricia simply leans toward it. The dog rapidly learned what she wanted because the signal was naturally understandable. In other words, Patricia is able to speak the dog's language.

Patricia McConnell, Ph.D. is a Certified Applied Animal Behaviorist and an

20 Adjunct Assistant Professor at the University of Wisconsin, Madison. She runs a highly successful dog training business and hosts a nationally syndicated radio show on applied animal behavior. Her success comes from this key insight: it is vital to take into account the natural behavior of an animal in order to communicate with it effectively.

25 Auditory communication has been one of her main interests. For an undergraduate honors project, she analyzed the voice and whistle commands handlers give to sheepherding dogs to tell them to walk toward the sheep, circle, and lie down. Handlers had told her that it's not important which whistle is used for which behavior as long as the sounds are easy to distinguish.

However, when Patricia sorted the sonographs (pictures of the sounds of whistles) into piles in categories based on what the command meant, her eyes showed her patterns that her ears had not caught: certain types of commands shared the same structure. As she was thinking about her data while riding horseback, she had another epiphany when she said, "Whooaa" to the skittish horse: long continuous notes are used to soothe many animals, and short, repeated notes (like clicking to a horse) are used to make them speed up. She remembers the joy of the discovery. "The clouds parted and the angels sang!"

A draft horse

In her dissertation, Patricia looked across cultures. She recorded more than 105 animal handlers that spoke 19 different languages. They were communicating with rodeo and draft horses, obedience and sled dogs, camels, yaks, guard geese, and cats, among others. Across these languages she found the same patterns: short, repeated notes meant speed up ("Kittykittykitty!"). Slow, unmodulated notes were used to soothe. Single, modulated notes ("Whoa!") were used to stop animals that were already active. Could it be that mammals are predisposed to respond in particular ways to these sounds? Patricia tested this idea by training Border collie and beagle puppies to respond to either four short tones with a rising frequency that meant "come" and one long tone with a descending frequency that meant "stay," or vice versa. As predicted, a command with four short tones was more effective than the long signal at getting dogs to approach and increasing their motor activity.

Sled dogs

Many people assume that they will automatically know the best way to communicate with their dog, but inter-species communication is more difficult than one might imagine. As Patricia says, "Imagine doing an ethnogram (an explanation of what animals are trying to say with their verbal and non-verbal language) on humans as an alien species and figuring out what something as simple as a smile means. It could be joy, nervousness, tension, or something else." A dog faces a similar problem as it tries to understand its trainer.

A yak

The business Patricia started with a hundred dollars when she had just finished her Ph.D. has grown into a success. She says applying her animal behavior degree in this way is more intellectually and emotionally challenging than she would ever have dreamed, and she is as proud of her abilities as an animal trainer as she is of her Ph.D. Days when she can solve a behavioral problem and prevent a dog from being put down (killed) are satisfying indeed.

Word Count: 734

Source: *Animal Behavior* (Drickamer, Vessey, and Jakob)

Timed Reading

Read "Secrets of Cross-species Communication" again. Read at a comfortable speed. Time your reading. Write your time in the Timed Reading Chart on page 236.

Start time: _____

End time: _____

My reading time: _____

"Communicate" comes from the Latin word com-mune which means "held in common." 🙠

After You Read

Comprehension

1. What is one secret of cross-species communication? _____

   _____

2. Patricia McConnell is certified to work with animals in a special occupation field. What is her

   field? _____

3. Along with teaching at the University of Wisconsin, Madison, Patricia McConnell has two

   other jobs. What are they? _____

   _____

4. What did Patricia McConnell learn from sonographs? _____

   _____

   _____

5. Explain in your own words what Patricia McConnell learned from her Ph.D. dissertation.

   _____

   _____

6. Why is training animals so satisfying to Patricia McConnell? _____

   _____

   _____

Talk About It
Discuss the following questions.
Is communicating with animals important?
Why or why not?

Reading 2: How Animals Signal Danger

Before You Read

Preview

A. The title of Reading 2 is "How Animals Signal Danger." What ways do you think that animals signal danger? Try to think of at least two different ways. Discuss your ideas with a partner.

B. Preview these words from the reading. Match each word with the correct definition below. Write the letter of the correct word on the line.

> a. excrete   d. predator   g. vocalizations
> b. mating   e. sedentary
> c. offspring   f. terrestrial

_____ **1.** not moving much

_____ **2.** coupling; pairing; sexual union

_____ **3.** an animal that hunts and eats other animals

_____ **4.** children

_____ **5.** animal or human sounds

_____ **6.** having to do with land, soil, or ground

_____ **7.** eliminate from the body

C. Preview these additional words from "How Animals Signal Danger." Match each word with the correct definition. Write the letter of the correct answer on the line.

Words	Definitions
_____ **1.** crushed	**a.** having to do with word meanings
_____ **2.** decoy	**b.** hurt; distressed; worried
_____ **3.** mutually	**c.** for both; shared
_____ **4.** semantically	**d.** broken
_____ **5.** stressed	**e.** imitation, especially a wooden duck painted to look like a real duck

Reading Skills

> # It's Your Turn
>
> Throughout this book, you've learned different strategies to preview a reading. Now it's time for you to think about the different ways, evaluate them, and decide which one(s) work best for you. So far, you've practiced:
>
> ▶ getting ready to read—finding good light and comfortable surroundings
>
> ▶ connecting with the topic
>
> ▶ using titles and headings
>
> ▶ using the introduction and conclusion
>
> ▶ brainstorming what you know about the topic
>
> ▶ previewing by looking at topic sentences
>
> ▶ using pictures and captions to preview a passage
>
> ▶ having an open mind
>
> When you have a passage to read, look it over and see which strategies you think will work well. Also, think about ways to preview a passage that haven't been covered in this book. For example, you might look the topic up on the Internet or ask friends what they know and think about the topic.

Practice

Preview Reading 2: "How Animals Signal Danger" (pages 221–224). Then answer the questions.

1. Which reading skill strategies did you use? _____

_____

_____

2. Based on what you did, what do you think the reading will be about?_____

_____

_____

3. Compare your answers with a partner. Which strategies were the same? _____

_____

_____

4. Which strategies were different?_____

_____

_____

5. Check the boxes below for how useful each reading skill stategy was for you.

Strategies	General Usefulness	Usefulness for Reading 2
Getting ready to read	☐ Very Useful ☐ Somewhat Useful ☐ Not Useful	☐ Very Useful ☐ Somewhat Useful ☐ Not Useful
Connecting with the topic	☐ Very Useful ☐ Somewhat Useful ☐ Not Useful	☐ Very Useful ☐ Somewhat Useful ☐ Not Useful
Using titles and headings	☐ Very Useful ☐ Somewhat Useful ☐ Not Useful	☐ Very Useful ☐ Somewhat Useful ☐ Not Useful
Using the introduction and conclusion	☐ Very Useful ☐ Somewhat Useful ☐ Not Useful	☐ Very Useful ☐ Somewhat Useful ☐ Not Useful
Brainstorming what you know about the topic	☐ Very Useful ☐ Somewhat Useful ☐ Not Useful	☐ Very Useful ☐ Somewhat Useful ☐ Not Useful
Previewing by looking at topic sentences	☐ Very Useful ☐ Somewhat Useful ☐ Not Useful	☐ Very Useful ☐ Somewhat Useful ☐ Not Useful
Having an open mind	☐ Very Useful ☐ Somewhat Useful ☐ Not Useful	☐ Very Useful ☐ Somewhat Useful ☐ Not Useful
Your idea(s)		

As you read, think about this question:
▶ How do animals signal danger?

🎧 How Animals Signal Danger

"Passing on your left," say bicycle riders as they pass you.
"Heads up," yells a construction worker on the job.
"Fore!" shouts a golfer as she swings.
"Hot! Don't touch," says a parent to a child.

5   All these expressions are used to tell the listener about danger. Humans generally use specific words to warn about different kinds of danger, but it is important for every species to have ways to let other members of their group know about danger.

African blue monkey

10 Vocalizations

Animals use vocalizations and chemicals to alert group members to danger. Although male calls (of romance and territory) vary greatly both within and among similar species, alarm vocalizations tend to be very similar. In fact, members of 15 species that live together, and that are endangered by the same predators, benefit mutually by minimizing divergence in alarm vocalizations. For example, 20 Marler (1973) was unable to tell the difference between the "chirp" alarm calls of African blue monkeys (*Crecopithecus mitis*) and those of red-tailed monkeys 25 (*C. ascanius*), whereas it was easy

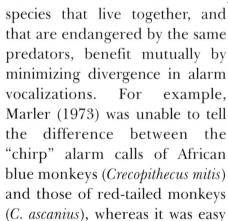

Red-tailed monkey

Vervet monkey

for him to differentiate the male mating calls of two species—in fact, they differed greatly. In other words, the danger calls were similar, but the mating calls were very different.

Vervet monkeys (*Chlorocebus aethiops*) communicate semantically by using 30 different signals to warn about different dangers to their environment. Group

members climb trees when they hear alarm calls, which are given in response to leopards. They look up when they hear eagle alarms, and they look down when they hear snake alarms. Young vervets give alarm calls in response to a variety of ani-
35 mals, and their ability to classify predators and give appropriate alarm calls improves with age.

Chemicals

Both invertebrates (animals without backbones) and vertebrates (animals with backbones) produce chemical alarm sub-
40 stances. Sea urchins of the species *Diadema antillarum* move rapidly away from an area containing a crushed member of their own species (Snyder and Snyder, 1970). Earthworms (*Lumbricus terrestris*) also produce alarm pheromones (Ressler et. al., 1968). (Pheromones are chemical substances that animals secrete.
45 These secretions always get the same response from animals of the same species.) Mice and rats excrete a substance in their urine when they are given electrical shocks, are beaten up by another animal, or otherwise stressed. This substance acts as an alarm and may cause others to avoid the area (Rottman and
50 Snowden, 1972).

Who Benefits from Alarm Calls?

Tracking the evolution of alarm calls presents a challenge to biologists because such signals seem unlikely to benefit the caller. Sherman (1977) studied individually marked Belding's
55 ground squirrels (*Spermophilus beldingi*), and found that whenever a terrestrial predator (such as a weasel or a coyote) was spotted, the calling squirrel stared directly at the predator while sounding the alarm.

This conspicuously calling squirrel, a lactating female, is more
60 likely to be attacked by a predator than is a noncaller. Nearby squirrels benefit since they can remain hidden or take cover. Females with mothers, sisters, or offspring in the area are most likely to call.

Sherman suggested many hypotheses to explain this behav-

Sea urchin

Earthworm

Ground squirrel

Coyote

ior, two of which we will discuss. First, the predator may abandon the hunt once it is spotted by the potential prey. (In this hypothesis, the caller is behaving selfishly.) Second, others in the area may benefit from the warning, even though the caller may be harmed. (In this hypothesis, the caller is behaving altruistically—doing it for the good of others.) Sherman demonstrated that callers attract predators and are more likely to be attacked after calling, and thus they are not behaving selfishly.

Because he kept records on mothers and offspring, Sherman knew that the males leave the area several months after birth and that the females are sedentary and breed near their birthplaces. He also found that adult and yearling females are more likely to call than would be expected by chance, and males are less likely to do so. Furthermore, females with female relatives in the area (such as mothers or sisters, but not necessarily with offspring) call more frequently in the presence of a predator than those with no female relatives living nearby. Sherman concluded that the most likely function of the alarm call is to warn family members. In other words, the squirrel herself did not benefit from making the alarm call, but it did help her family and near relatives.

Using Body Language to Show Danger

Models have been useful in the study of the function of alarm calls, as seen in work on pastures of brent geese (*Branta bernicla*) (Inglis and Issacson, 1978). When alarmed by sudden auditory or visual stimuli, geese adopt the extreme head-up posture.

Dark-bellied brent goose (left); pale-bellied brent goose (right)

When "flocks" of decoys were placed in grain fields where geese had been caus-
ing damage, real flocks' responses depended on the decoys' postures. In general,
the real flocks avoided fields with a high proportion of extreme head-up decoys,
90 while they were attracted to the fields with mostly head-down decoys.

*Models of brent geese postures. When "flocks" of geese models are placed in grain fields, real geese avoid
fields containing models in the extreme head-up (alarm) posture.*

Like humans, animals can alert each other in times of danger. While our
knowledge of animal communication is limited, it nonetheless offers a complex
and fascinating window into the natural world.

Word Count: 919

Source: *Animal Behavior* (Drickamer, Vessey, and Jakob)

Timed Reading

Read "How Animals Signal Danger" again.
Read at a comfortable speed. Time your your
reading. Write your time in the Timed
Reading Chart on page 236.

Start time: _____

End time: _____

My reading time: _____

After You Read

Reading Skills

Using Notes to Write a Summary

So far, you have learned different ways to take notes, such as writing an outline or using different kinds of graphic organizers. Good notes are important when you write a summary of a reading. A summary is a shorter version of the reading written in your own words. Writing a summary is a good way to remember what you have read, and it can help you prepare for tests and write papers.

A summary has these characteristics:

▶ It is shorter than the original reading.

▶ It tells the main ideas.

▶ It does not give details and/or specific examples.

▶ It does not give opinions about the reading.

▶ It mentions the author and/or title of the reading.

Here's a summary of Reading 1, "Secrets of Cross-species Communication" on pages 214–216:

"Secrets of Cross-species Communication" describes the research Patricia McConnell has done with dogs, horses, camels, and other animals. She learned that the best way for humans to communicate with animals is to use techniques based on the animals' natural behavior. McConnell is particularly interested in auditory communication. She found that short, repeated sounds mean "speed up" and slow sounds work to soothe animals. Her ability to solve animal communication problems has saved many animals' lives.

When you have finished your summary, reread what you have written, and revise if necessary.

Practice

In this chapter, instead of answering comprehension questions, take notes on and write a summary of "How Animals Signal Danger." Compare your summary with a partner. Use the following questions.

1. What format did you each choose to take your notes?
2. How long is your summary? How long is your partner's summary?
3. Did you each include all the main ideas?
4. Did you each include only the main ideas?
5. Does the summary mention the title of the reading?
6. Is there any information that should not be in the summary? If so, why? Is there any information missing that should be in the summary? If so, what?

Vocabulary

A. Here are some more words from "How Animals Signal Danger." Find them in the reading and circle them.

Nouns	Verbs	Adjective
divergence prey	abandon chirp spotted	potential

B. Now use them to complete the sentences.

1. Birds _____. This word for short, song-like noises is also used to describe monkey sounds.

2. Eagles catch _____ such as squirrels. They use their excellent eyesight to find small animals to eat.

3. It is better for animals of one species not to have any _____ in alarm calls. If their alarm calls sound alike, they are more likely to survive

4. Most predators do not _____ a hunt if the animal they are hunting sees them. They usually keep hunting it and don't give up.

5. Once an eagle sees a monkey, it will usually pursue its _____ meal until it captures it.

6. The monkey _____ the snake and ran up the tree. Because he saw it, he let out loud "snake danger" cries.

Talk About It

Discuss these questions.

1. What words or sounds do you use to signal danger?
2. Describe a time when you saw an animal in danger. What happened? What did the animal do?

What sounds do you use...?

I . . .

Expressions

> ### Collocations for Talking about Animal Communication
>
> Collocations are words that are frequently used together. Here are some collocations that relate to the study of animal communication.
>
> | | |
> |---|---|
> | **be expected by** | **gets the message** |
> | **benefit from** | **keep records on** |
> | **communicate with** | **in response to** |
> | **excrete a substance** | **stared directly at** |
>
> When you learn collocations, notice how they are used in a sentence. Also, notice the entire expression. For example, notice which verbs and prepositions are in it.
>
> **Examples:**
>
> The researchers wondered how the squirrels could **benefit from** looking directly at the predator.
>
> Sherman found that adult and yearling female squirrels are more likely to call than would **be expected by** chance.

Practice

A. Find and underline the collocations in the box above in "Secrets of Cross-species Communication" and "How Animals Signal Danger."

B. Now use some of them to complete the sentences.

1. Researchers were surprised to see that the animal _____ its predator because normally it would have run away.

2. People always want to _____ their pets, so they talk to them frequently.

3. Patricia swings her hips toward the dog when he jumps at her. You can tell the dog quickly

   _____ because it sits back on its haunches.

4. To compare early results with later results, the researchers _____ every experiment they do in special notebooks.

5. _____ seeing a leopard, most animals give a warning cry.

6. Some animals _____, which acts as an alarm to other animals in the area.

Internet Research

Finding Specific Information on a Webpage

You can find a specific word or phrase quickly on a webpage using the *Find* function of your browser. It's especially useful on pages that have a great deal of text on them. To do this, open a webpage and select the *Edit* pull-down menu in your browser. Select *Find*. In the *Find* textbox, write the word or phrase you want to locate on the page. (Note: You don't need to use capital letters if it's a name.) Then click the *Find* button, and the first instance of the word or phrase on the page will be highlighted. To find the word or phrase again on the page, select *Find Again* from the *Edit* pull-down menu and the next instance will be highlighted.

Practice

Practice using the *Find* function to locate more examples of animal communication on the Internet. First, use a search engine (such as Google) to do a search for "animal communication" and an animal you want to know more about (such as cats, parrots, or elephants). Then choose a webpage about animal communication and use *Find* to locate on the page information on a particular animal. Collect information on one of the following animals, or try your own words and phrases:

Animals		
cats	elephants	sea lions
camels	guard geese	sled dogs
dolphins	horses	yaks

Tell the class about your *Find* experience and your results.

Write About It

Write a paragraph about animal communication. Choose one of these topics:

▶ Write about the results of your Internet research on animal communication.
▶ Do animals communicate as well as people? Explain your opinion.

Use five words and expressions from this chapter. Also, try to use your Internet research.

On Your Own

Project

Give an oral presentation on communication, either individually or in small groups.

Step 1: Prepare

Decide on a topic. For your topic, choose something about animal communication, human communication, or the interaction of animal and human communication. You may wish to talk about how people in the class communicate danger verbally and non-verbally, or you may wish to present your Internet research. Your teacher will give you a time limit, so be sure your topic will fit within the limit. Brainstorm ideas, do research if necessary, and outline the content.

Practice your presentations in groups.

Step 2: Give Your Presentation

Give your presentation. Have your classmates evaluate your presentation. You may want to create a form for them to fill out. Decide what kind of input your would like. The form could look something like this:

Speaker _____			Evaluator _____	
Presentation	**Good**	**OK**	**Needs Improvement**	**Comments**
1. The speaker was energetic, did not read the speech, and maintained eye contact.				
2. The speaker provided new information, and I learned something from the presentation.				
3. The speaker repeated important points.				
4. The speaker had good visual aids.				
5. The speaker could answer questions from the audience.				

Step 3: Follow-Up

Evaluate your own speech. How did you do? What was good? What needs improvement?

Wrap Up

How Much Do You Remember?

Check your new knowledge. In this chapter you learned facts, words, and expressions. You also learned reading skills and you practiced writing. Complete the following to check what you remember.

1. What kinds of sounds make animals speed up? _____

    _____

2. Why can a smile be difficult to interpret? _____

    _____

3. How do vervet monkeys respond to eagle alarms and snake alarms? _____

    _____

    _____

4. Are the alarm cries of Belding's ground squirrels selfish or not? Why? _____

    _____

    _____

5. Use *gets the message* in a sentence. _____

    _____

6. Why is it useful to summarize a reading assignment? _____

    _____

    _____

7. How can you find specific information on a webpage? _____

    _____

    _____

Second Timed Readings

Now reread "Secrets of Cross-species Communication" and "How Animals Signal Danger." Time each reading separately. Write your times in the Timed Reading Chart on page 236.

Crossword Puzzle

Complete the crossword puzzle to practice some words and expressions from this chapter.

CLUES

Across →
   1. Joints below the waist and above the thighs that help move the legs
   4. A wooden duck painted to look like a real duck
   8. Warn
   9. Children
   10. Having to do with a way of acting
   11. Very important

Down ↓
   2. Make calm
   3. Enemy
   5. Possible
   6. A dog's tail does this when he's happy.
   7. A sudden realization

Timed Reading Chart

Use this chart to keep track of your reading times.

CHAPTER 3: Business Communication

Email   **Page 54**

First Reading   **Second Reading**

Start time: _____   Start time: _____

End time: _____   End time: _____

My reading time: _____   My reading time: _____

Making an Oral Presentation   **Page 60**

First Reading   **Second Reading**

Start time: _____   Start time: _____

End time: _____   End time: _____

My reading time: _____   My reading time: _____

CHAPTER 4: Business Ethics

Ethics: An Introduction   **Page 76**

First Reading   **Second Reading**

Start time: _____   Start time: _____

End time: _____   End time: _____

My reading time: _____   My reading time: _____

Ethics in Business: Hewlett-Packard   **Page 82**

First Reading   **Second Reading**

Start time: _____   Start time: _____

End time: _____   End time: _____

My reading time: _____   My reading time: _____

Timed Reading Chart

Use this chart to keep track of your reading times.

UNIT 3   FILM STUDIES

CHAPTER 5: History of Film

Film History Timeline: 1893 to the Present   **Page 100**

First Reading

Start time: _____

End time: _____

My reading time: _____

Second Reading

Start time: _____

End time: _____

My reading time: _____

The New Hollywood   **Page 107**

First Reading

Start time: _____

End time: _____

My reading time: _____

Second Reading

Start time: _____

End time: _____

My reading time: _____

CHAPTER 6: Genre Films

A Review of *Star Wars*   **Page 122**

First Reading

Start time: _____

End time: _____

My reading time: _____

Second Reading

Start time: _____

End time: _____

My reading time: _____

Genre Films   **Page 128**

First Reading

Start time: _____

End time: _____

My reading time: _____

Second Reading

Start time: _____

End time: _____

My reading time: _____

UNIT 4 HUMAN GEOGRAPHY

CHAPTER 7: Population

Population Trends

First Reading

Start time: _____

End time: _____

My reading time: _____

Second Reading

Start time: _____

End time: _____

My reading time: _____

Page 146

Nations of Immigrants

First Reading

Start time: _____

End time: _____

My reading time: _____

Second Reading

Start time: _____

End time: _____

My reading time: _____

Page 152

CHAPTER 8: People and the Environment

The Mystery of Easter Island

First Reading

Start time: _____

End time: _____

My reading time: _____

Second Reading

Start time: _____

End time: _____

My reading time: _____

Page 168

Cultural Ecology

First Reading

Start time: _____

End time: _____

My reading time: _____

Second Reading

Start time: _____

End time: _____

My reading time: _____

Page 174

Timed Reading Chart

Use this chart to keep track of your reading times.

UNIT 5 BIOLOGY

CHAPTER 9: Cloning

Reading 1: Cloned Cat is No Copycat   **Page 192**

First Reading	Second Reading
Start time: _____	Start time: _____
End time: _____	End time: _____
My reading time: _____	My reading time: _____

Reading 2: The Ethics of Cloning   **Page 198**

First Reading	Second Reading
Start time: _____	Start time: _____
End time: _____	End time: _____
My reading time: _____	My reading time: _____

CHAPTER 10: Animal Communication

Reading 1: Secrets of Cross-species Communication   **Page 214**

First Reading	Second Reading
Start time: _____	Start time: _____
End time: _____	End time: _____
My reading time: _____	My reading time: _____

Reading 2: How Animals Signal Danger   **Page 221**

First Reading	Second Reading
Start time: _____	Start time: _____
End time: _____	End time: _____
My reading time: _____	My reading time: _____

Vocabulary Index

Chapter 1

authority
barrier
be exercising good judgment
bias
conformism
convincing arguments
covering
draw appropriate conclusions
drop
elements
find fault
herd instinct
objectively
outgrow
overrate
personal prejudices
relate
section
stereotype
tendency
trait
unconsciously
unreasonable
unwarranted
upcoming

Chapter 2

abandon
affirmation
"aha" experience
assess
be in a creative state of mind
be in a rut
breakthrough
(break) broke with tradition
criteria
decoding
extend the boundaries of
generate ideas
imprisoned by
inquisitive
is fundamental to
judging the merit of
mental blocks
multidimensional
nonconformist
no-risk path

open frame of mind
open your mind to
perceive
perceptual filters
play it safe
to putter
reluctant
stepping-stones
to strive to
subconscious
suspend judgment
sustained
take themselves too seriously
tolerate ambiguity
unlock your mind

Chapter 3

absorb information
allotted
assemblers
attractive
backup
brainstorm ideas
CEO
concise
conventions
convey
deliver your presentation
distinctive
distribute
efficient
eliminate
ends on a positive note
fear of speaking
gender
have stage fright
interaction
keep the audience focused
loosen
manage
master
niceties
pace
persuasive
retirement
self-confident
urgency
vehicle

via email
well-groomed

Chapter 4

a/the decision making process
absolute
adhere to
avoiding conflicts of interest
be concerned with social/environmental responsibility
bribes
compliance with
confront
consistent with
core values
develop a code of ethics
financial sums
fosters
has/have a stake in the outcome
honoring confidential information
impact
initiative
integrity
intentional
layoffs
partitions
perspective
profit-sharing plan
shifted
stock-purchase plan
teamwork
the basis of moral values
through consensus

Chapter 5

achieved acclaim with
aesthetics
atmospheric
commercially distributed
consisted of (a single shot)
conventional
(a) critical success
dazzling
disrupt
distorted
divisiveness
Expressionism
(a) financial success

found success in (Hollywood)
have their roots in (the early days)
Impressionism
inexplicable
ingenuity
innovative
intrigue
led to (a series of discoveries)
merge
narrative
narrative structure
Neorealism
pays homage to (the classical
Hollywood movie)
perversely
prototype
rebel against (the establishment)
repulse
returned to his roots in (China)
satire
stunningly photographed
Surrealism
tight editing
understated
via flashbacks
winning recognition

Chapter 6

anarchy
assume
bully
cocky
crooked
deceptively
fading sunset
fastidious
fixed camera
gutter
hovers over
inspirations
knock-down, drag-out barroom brawl
latent instincts
melded
(be his) own man
to pan
personal code
prolonged chase
quest
reaffirmed
redemption
resolution

rugged individualist
setting
shorthand
soap opera
space opera
surround sound
underdog
vulnerable point
watershed

Chapter 7

affected by
anticipated
be a magnet for
collective
colonists
comprise
conceal
density of settlement
descent
disparities
distributions of people
domination
ejects
enmity
estimated
famines
fertility
incidences
interpretation
mortality
overwhelmed
policies of exclusion
policies on immigration
population projections
potential
rate of growth
recruited
reversal
right of admittance
sex distribution
to stem
trend

Chapter 8

abound
annihilation
broke out
(be) carried on by
clear off
the cultural landscape

decimated
deforestation
desolate
dried up
enhanced
exterminated
habitable
hunted to extinction
immense
knock (something) down
leeched
massive
migrated to
millennia
obliterated by
quarries
ran out of
reclaim
sediment
tangible
timber
turbulent
wasteland

Chapter 9

at the heart of
cloudy
creates fear
defense
déluge
embryos
espoused
euthanized
exploit
gene therapy
get successful results
has been neutered
hereditary disorders
human genome
in the long run/term
in the short run/term
infertile
misperception
profound
raises (profound) issues
resistance
resurrect
scientific advances
sequenced
sparked
strip ourselves of

supposition
surrounding
the (genetic) dice were rolled for all
of us
turn out as
variation
vindicates

Chapter 10

abandon
be expected by
behavioral
benefit from
chirp
communicate with
divergence
epiphany
excrete
frequency
gets the message
handlers
hips
in response to
keep records on
keep the audience focused
mating
offspring
potential
predator
prey
sedentary
soothe
spotted
stared directly at
syndicated
terrestrial
vital
vocalizations
wags
whoa

Skills Index

Population, 146–148
Problem solving, 30–31, 36–38

Pre-reading Questions/Activities, 5,
6, 13, 27, 28, 33, 34, 51, 52,
57, 58, 73, 74, 79, 97, 98,
105–106, 119, 120, 126, 127,
143, 144, 150, 151, 165, 166,
172, 189, 190, 197, 211, 212,
218

Skills
Connecting with the topic, 57–58
Fact (vs. opinion), 111
Forming an opinion, 202–203
Getting ready to read, 14
Graphic organizers, 40–41, 87, 157
Having an open mind, 173
Identifying cause and effect, 178–179
Identifying facts and opinions, 111
Identifying similarities and differ-
ences, 8, 133
Identifying the main idea, 18
Identifying supporting ideas, 18
Inferences, 86–87
Making inferences, 86–87
Opinions, 202–203
Outlining, 40–41, 136
Paraphrasing, 64–65
Previewing,
Putting it all together, 126–127,
195–196
Using captions (and pictures), 150
Using conclusions (and introduc-
tions), 80–81
Using headings, 33–34,
Using introductions (and conclu-
sions), 80–81
Using pictures (and captions), 150
Using titles, 33–34
Using topic sentences, 105
Summarizing, 225

Taking notes, 40–41, 225
Using your own strategies, 219–220

Surveys,
Research, 23, 115
Short, 4, 26, 50, 72, 96, 118, 142,
164, 188, 210

Timed readings, 11, 17, 31, 38, 55,
63, 77, 85, 103, 109, 123, 131,
148, 155, 170, 177, 193, 200,
216, 224
Charts, 232–236

Vocabulary and Vocabulary Skills
Animals (communication), 213, 218,
226, 227
Business,
Communication, 53, 59, 66
Ethics, 75, 79, 88
Cloning, 191, 197, 204
Communication,
Animal, 218, 226, 227 (expressions
for)
Business, 53, 59, 66
Cross-species, 213, 218
Critical thinking, 7, 13, 20
Cultural ecology, 172, 180
Environment, 167, 172
Ethics, 75, 79, 88
Film,
Genre, 121, 134
History, 99, 112
Immigrants, 151, 158
Population, 145
Problem solving, 29, 35, 42

Writing Topics
Business, 68, 90
Cloning, 206
Communication (animals and
human), 228

Critical thinking, 22
Emails, 68
Environment, 182
Ethics, 90
Film history, 114
Immigration experience, 160
Lost civilization, 182
Movies reviews, 136
Nervousness, 68
Population growth, 160
Problem solving, 44
Reading habits, 22
Reviews (movies), 136

Writing Types
Analyzing,
Movie reviews, 136
Comparing,
Communication, 228
Describing,
Animal communication, 228
Communication (animal), 228
Critical thinking, 22
Environment, 182
Ethics, 90
Favorite place to read, 22
Feelings about oral presentations,
68
Film history, 114
First movie-going experience, 114
Immigration experience, 160
Lost civilization, 182
Population growth, 160
Problems, 44
Explaining,
Preservation of environment, 182
Techniques to overcome nervous-
ness, 68
Opinion,
Cloning, 206
Reviewing, 136 (movies)

Academic Word List

To help you increase your vocabulary we have included Sublist One of the most common words on the Academic Word List, a list compiled by Averil Coxhead. To view the entire list, go to Averil Coxhead's AWL website (http://language.massey.ac.nz/staff/awl/index.shtml).

Each word in italics is the most frequently occurring member of the word family in the academic corpus. For example, *analysis* is the most common form of the word family *analyse*.

analyse
  analysed
  analyser
  analysers
  analyses
  analysing
  analysis
  analyst
  analysts
  analytic
  analytical
  analytically
  analyze
  analyzed
  analyzes
  analyzing
approach
  approachable
  approached
  approaches
  approaching
  unapproachable
area
  areas
assess
  assessable
  assessed
  assesses
  assessing
  assessment
  assessments
  reassess
  reassessed
  reassessing

reassessment
unassessed
assume
  assumed
  assumes
  assuming
  assumption
  assumptions
authority
  authoritative
  authorities
available
  availability
  unavailable
benefit
  beneficial
  beneficiary
  beneficiaries
  benefited
  benefiting
  benefits
concept
  conception
  concepts
  conceptual
  conceptualisation
  conceptualise
  conceptualised
  conceptualises
  conceptualising
  conceptually
consist
  consisted
  consistency
  consistent

consistently
consisting
consists
inconsistencies
inconsistency
inconsistent
constitute
  constituencies
  constituency
  constituent
  constituents
  constituted
  constitutes
  constituting
  constitution
  constitutions
  constitutional
  constitutionally
  constitutive
  unconstitutional
context
  contexts
  contextual
  contextualise
  contextualised
  contextualising
  uncontextualised
  contextualize
  contextualized
  contextualizing
  uncontextualized
contract
  contracted
  contracting

contractor
contractors
contracts
create
  created
  creates
  creating
  creation
  creations
  creative
  creatively
  creativity
  creator
  creators
  recreate
  recreated
  recreates
  recreating
data
define
  definable
  defined
  defines
  defining
  definition
  definitions
  redefine
  redefined
  redefines
  redefining
  undefined
derive
  derivation
  derivations
  derivative
  derivatives
  derived
  derives
  deriving
distribute
  distributed
  distributing
  distribution

distributional
distributions
distributive
distributor
distributors
redistribute
redistributed
redistributes
redistributing
redistribution
economy
  economic
  economical
  economically
  economics
  economies
  economist
  economists
  uneconomical
environment
  environmental
  environmentalist
  environmentalists
  environmentally
  environments
establish
  disestablish
  disestablished
  disestablishes
  disestablishing
  disestablishment
  established
  establishes
  establishing
  establishment
  establishments
estimate
  estimated
  estimates
  estimating
  estimation
  estimations
  over-estimate

overestimate
overestimated
overestimates
overestimating
underestimate
underestimated
underestimates
underestimating
evident
  evidenced
  evidence
  evidential
  evidently
export
  exported
  exporter
  exporters
  exporting
  exports
factor
  factored
  factoring
  factors
finance
  financed
  finances
  financial
  financially
  financier
  financiers
  financing
formula
  formulae
  formulas
  formulate
  formulated
  formulating
  formulation
  formulations
  reformulate
  reformulated
  reformulating

reformulation
reformulations
function
  functional
  functionally
  functioned
  functioning
  functions
identify
  identifiable
  identification
  identified
  identifies
  identifying
  identities
  identity
  unidentifiable
income
  incomes
indicate
  indicated
  indicates
  indicating
  indication
  indications
  indicative
  indicator
  indicators
individual
  individualised
  individuality
  individualism
  individualist
  individualists
  individualistic
  individually
  individuals
interpret
  interpretation
  interpretations
  interpretative
  interpreted
  interpreting

interpretive
interprets
misinterpret
misinterpretation
misinterpretations
misinterpreted
misinterpreting
misinterprets
reinterpret
reinterpreted
reinterprets
reinterpreting
reinterpretation
reinterpretations
involve
  involved
  involvement
  involves
  involving
  uninvolved
issue
  issued
  issues
  issuing
labour
  labor
  labored
  labors
  laboured
  labouring
  labours
legal
  illegal
  illegality
  illegally
  legality
  legally
legislate
  legislated
  legislates
  legislating
  legislation
  legislative

legislator
legislators
legislature
major
  majorities
  majority
method
  methodical
  methodological
  methodologies
  methodology
  methods
occur
  occurred
  occurrence
  occurrences
  occurring
  occurs
  reoccur
  reoccurred
  reoccurring
  reoccurs
percent
  percentage
  percentages
period
  periodic
  periodical
  periodically
  periodicals
  periods
policy
  policies
principle
  principled
  principles
  unprincipled
proceed
  procedural
  procedure
  procedures
  proceeded
  proceeding

proceedings
proceeds
process
processed
processes
processing
require
required
requirement
requirements
requires
requiring
research
researched
researcher
researchers
researches
researching
respond
responded
respondent
respondents
responding
responds
response
responses
responsive
responsiveness
unresponsive
role
roles

section
sectioned
sectioning
sections
sector
sectors
significant
insignificant
insignificantly
significance
significantly
signified
signifies
signify
signifying
similar
dissimilar
similarities
similarity
similarly
source
sourced
sources
sourcing
specific
specifically
specification
specifications
specificity
specifics
structure
restructure
restructured

restructures
restructuring
structural
structurally
structured
structures
structuring
unstructured
theory
theoretical
theoretically
theories
theorist
theorists
vary
invariable
invariably
variability
variable
variables
variably
variance
variant
variants
variation
variations
varied
varies
varying

Frequency Word List

Below are the most common words in English. This list is compiled by Edward Bernard Fry, Jacqueline E. Kress, and Dona Lee Fountoukidis.

These most commonly used words are ranked by frequency. The first 25 make up about one-third of all printed material in English. The first 100 make up about one-half of all written material, and the first 300 make up about sixty-five percent of all written material in English.

1. the	36. we	71. two
2. of	37. when	72. more
3. and	38. your	73. write
4. a	39. can	74. go
5. to	40. said	75. see
6. in	41. there	76. number
7. is	42. use	77. no
8. you	43. an	78. way
9. that	44. each	79. could
10. it	45. which	80. people
11. he	46. she	81. my
12. was	47. do	82. than
13. for	48. how	83. first
14. on	49. their	84. water
15. are	50. if	85. been
16. as	51. will	86. call
17. with	52. up	87. who
18. his	53. other	88. oil
19. they	54. about	89. its
20. I	55. out	90. now
21. at	56. many	91. find
22. be	57. then	92. long
23. this	58. them	93. down
24. have	59. these	94. day
25. from	60. so	95. did
26. or	61. some	96. get
27. one	62. her	97. come
28. had	63. would	98. made
29. by	64. make	99. may
30. word	65. like	100. part
31. but	66. him	101. over
32. not	67. into	102. new
33. what	68. time	103. sound
34. all	69. has	104. take
35. were	70. look	105. only

106. little	150. small	194. found
107. work	151. set	195. study
108. know	152. put	196. still
109. place	153. end	197. learn
110. year	154. does	198. should
111. live	155. another	199. America
112. me	156. well	200. world
113. back	157. large	201. high
114. give	158. must	202. every
115. most	159. big	203. near
116. very	160. even	204. add
117. after	161. such	205. food
118. thing	162. because	206. between
119. our	163. turn	207. own
120. just	164. here	208. below
121. name	165. why	209. country
122. good	166. ask	210. plant
123. sentence	167. went	211. last
124. man	168. men	212. school
125. think	169. read	213. father
126. say	170. need	214. keep
127. great	171. land	215. tree
128. where	172. different	216. never
129. help	173. home	217. start
130. through	174. us	218. city
131. much	175. move	219. earth
132. before	176. try	220. eye
133. line	177. kind	221. light
134. right	178. hand	222. thought
135. too	179. picture	223. head
136. mean	180. again	224. under
137. old	181. change	225. story
138. any	182. off	226. saw
139. same	183. play	227. left
140. tell	184. spell	228. don't
141. boy	185. air	229. few
142. follow	186. away	230. while
143. came	187. animal	231. along
144. want	188. house	232. might
145. show	189. point	233. close
146. also	190. page	234. something
147. around	191. letter	235. seem
148. form	192. mother	236. next
149. three	193. answer	237. hard

238. open	282. far	326. order
239. example	283. Indian	327. red
240. begin	284. really	328. door
241. life	285. almost	329. sure
242. always	286. let	330. become
243. those	287. above	331. top
244. both	288. girl	332. ship
245. paper	289. sometimes	333. across
246. together	290. mountain	334. today
247. got	291. cut	335. during
248. group	292. young	336. short
249. often	293. talk	337. better
250. run	294. soon	338. best
251. important	295. list	339. however
252. until	296. song	340. low
253. children	297. being	341. hours
254. side	298. leave	342. black
255. feet	299. family	343. products
256. car	300. it's	344. happened
257. mile	301. body	345. whole
258. night	302. music	346. measure
259. walk	303. color	347. remember
260. white	304. stand	348. early
261. sea	305. sun	349. waves
262. began	306. questions	350. reached
263. grow	307. fish	351. listen
264. took	308. area	352. wind
265. river	309. mark	353. rock
266. four	310. dog	354. space
267. carry	311. horse	355. covered
268. state	312. birds	356. fast
269. once	313. problem	357. several
270. book	314. complete	358. hold
271. hear	315. room	359. himself
272. stop	316. knew	360. toward
273. without	317. since	361. five
274. second	318. ever	362. step
275. later	319. piece	363. morning
276. miss	320. told	364. passed
277. idea	321. usually	365. vowel
278. enough	322. didn't	366. true
279. eat	323. friends	367. hundred
280. face	324. easy	368. against
281. watch	325. heard	369. pattern

370. numeral	414. person	458. force
371. table	415. became	459. brought
372. north	416. shown	460. understand
373. slowly	417. minutes	461. warm
374. money	418. strong	462. common
375. map	419. verb	463. bring
376. farm	420. stars	464. explain
377. pulled	421. front	465. dry
378. draw	422. feel	466. though
379. voice	423. fact	467. language
380. seen	424. inches	468. shape
381. cold	425. street	469. deep
382. cried	426. decided	470. thousands
383. plan	427. contain	471. yes
384. notice	428. course	472. clear
385. south	429. surface	473. equation
386. sing	430. produce	474. yet
387. war	431. building	475. government
388. ground	432. ocean	476. filled
389. fall	433. class	477. heat
390. king	434. note	478. full
391. town	435. nothing	479. hot
392. I'll	436. rest	480. check
393. unit	437. carefully	481. object
394. figure	438. scientists	482. am
395. certain	439. inside	483. rule
396. field	440. wheels	484. among
397. travel	441. stay	485. noun
398. wood	442. green	486. power
399. fire	443. known	487. cannot
400. upon	444. island	488. able
401. done	445. week	489. six
402. English	446. less	490. size
403. road	447. machine	491. dark
404. halt	448. base	492. ball
405. ten	449. ago	493. material
406. fly	450. stood	494. special
407. gave	451. plane	495. heavy
408. box	452. system	496. fine
409. finally	453. behind	497. pair
410. wait	454. ran	498. circle
411. correct	455. round	499. include
412. oh	456. boat	500. built
413. quickly	457. game	

Text Credits

p. 15 Adapted from *Critical Thinking: A Student's Introduction* by Gregory Bassham, William Irwin, Henry Nardone, and James M. Wallace, 2005. Reprinted by permission of the McGraw-Hill Companies. pp. 30, 36 Adapted from *Peak Performance: Success in College and Beyond*, 4e by Sharon K. Ferrett, 2002. Reprinted by permission of the McGraw-Hill Companies. p. 54 Adapted from *Management Communication: Principals and Practices*, 2e, by Michael E. Hattersley and Linda M. McJannet, 2004. Reprinted by permission of the McGraw-Hill Companies. p. 60 Adapted from *Communicating in the Workplace*, 6e, by Margaret Dombeck, Sue Camp, and Marilyn Satterwhite, 2003. Reprinted by permission of the McGraw-Hill Companies. p. 76 Adapted from *The Art of Leadership* by George Manning and Kent Curtis, 2003. Reprinted by permission of the McGraw-Hill Companies. p. 76 Adapted from *Perspectives in Business Ethics*, 2e, by Laura P. Hartman, 2001. Reprinted by permission of the McGraw-Hill Companies. p. 82 Adapted from *Business Ethics*, 2e, by David J. Fritzsche, 2004. Reprinted by permission of the McGraw-Hill Companies. p. 100 Adapted from *Film Art: An Introduction* by David Bordwell, Kristin Thompson, 7e, 2004. Reprinted by permission of the McGraw-Hill Companies. p. 107 Adapted from *Making Sense of Movies: Filmmaking in the Hollywood Style* by Robert Henry Stanley, 2002. Reprinted by permission of the McGraw-Hill Companies. p. 122 Adapted movie review of "Star Wars" by Roger Ebert, from *The Great Movies*, 2002. Roger Ebert © 2002 The Roger Ebert Company. Reprinted by permission of Universal Press Syndicate. All rights reserved. p. 128 Adapted from *The Art of Watching Films*, 6e, by Joe Boggs and Dennis W. Petrie, 2003. by permission of the McGraw-Hill Companies. pp. 146, 152, 174 From *Human Geography*, 8e, by Jerome D, Fellmann, Arthur Getis, Judith Getis, and Jon Malinowski, 2005. Reprinted by permission of the McGraw-Hill Companies. p. 168 Adapted from "Easter's End" by Jared Diamond, as appeared in *Discover*, Vol. 16, #08, August, 1995. Reprinted by permission of the author. p. 192 From "A Year Later: Cloned Cat is No Copycat" by Kristen Hays, *The Associated Press, Update*, Nov. 4th, 2003. © The Associated Press. All rights reserved. Reprinted with permission. p. 198 Adapted from *The Living World*, 3e, by George B. Johnson, 2003. Reprinted by permission of the McGraw-Hill Companies. p. 214, 221 Adapted from *Animal Behavior*, 5e, by Lee C. Drickamer, Stephen H. Vessey, and Elizabeth Jakob, 2001. Reprinted by permission of the McGraw-Hill Companies. p. 243 "Academic Word List Sublist One" by Averil Coxhead, as appeared on website www.language.massey.ac.nz/staff/awl/index.shtml. Reprinted by permission of Averil Coxhead. p. 247 From "Frequency Word List" from *The Reading Teacher's Book of Lists*, 4e by Edward Bernard Fry, Jacqueline E. Kress and Dona Lee Fountoukidis. Copyright © 2000. Reprinted with permission of John Wiley & Sons, Inc.

Photo Credits

From the Getty Images Royalty-Free Collection: p. 2; p. 48; p. 83; p. 94; p. 140; p. 142, right; p. 152; p. 164, left; p. 168; p. 169; p. 175; p. 177; p. 186; p. 197; p. 215, top; p. 215, middle.

From the CORBIS Royalty-Free Collection: p. 164, right; p. 199.

Other Images: p. 0, top left: Michelangelo Gratton/Getty Images; p. 0, top right: Stockbyte/Getty Images; p. 0, bottom left: Simon Taplin/Getty Images; p. 0, bottom right: Dougal Waters/Getty Images; p. 4, left: Christie's Images/CORBIS; p. 4, right: © Michael Newman/PhotoEdit; p. 8, left: © Michael Newman/PhotoEdit; p. 8, right: © Gary Conner/PhotoEdit; p. 15: Christie's Images/CORBIS; p. 17: Christopher D. Scott; p. 26, left: Mary Evans Picture Library; p. 26, right: McGraw-Hill Companies, Inc./Gary He, photographer; p. 29: © Michael Nicholson/CORBIS; p. 30: McGraw-Hill Companies, Inc./Gary He, photographer; p. 36: © Bettmann/CORBIS; p. 37: Mary Evans Picture Library; p. 50, left: © Ethan Miller/CORBIS; p. 50, right: © Marty Heitner/The Image Works; p. 54: © Ethan Miller/CORBIS; p. 60: © Marty Heitner/The Image Works; p. 72, left: Justin Sullivan/Getty Images; p. 72, right: © Bettmann/CORBIS; p. 76: © Bettmann/CORBIS; p. 82: AP/Wide World Photos; p. 84: Justin Sullivan/Getty Images; p. 96, left: Photo by Gaumont/Zuma Press; p. 96, right: New Line/Roger Birnbaum/The Kobal Collection/Marshak, Bob; p. 100, top: Melies/The Kobal Collection; p. 100, bottom: Photo by Gaumont/Zuma Press; p. 101, top: Photo by Edison/Zuma Press; p. 101, bottom: Prana-Film/The Kobal Collection; p. 102, top: Bunuel-Dali/The Kobal Collection; p. 102, bottom: © John Springer Collection/CORBIS; p. 103, left: Miramax/Buena Vista/The Kobal Collection; p. 103, right: Centenaire du Cinema/CORBIS SYGMA; p. 107: © Reuters/CORBIS; p. 108, top: Tri Star/The Kobal

Notes

Notes

Notes